KnOCK 'em DEaD

SECRETS & STRATEGIES
— FOR —
FIRST-TIME JOB SEEKERS

MARTIN YATE, CPC
New York Times bestselling author

A adamsmedia

AVON, MASSACHUSETTS

ACKNOWLEDGMENTS

I would like to thank the following people for their help in bringing *Knock 'em Dead: Secrets & Strategies for First-Time Job Seekers* to life: Karen Cooper at Adams Media for inviting me to do the book, and the erudite Peter Archer for managing the project with his usual editorial aplomb and gentle wit. William Yate for the sure editorial hand and copyediting skills that allowed us to bring in a great book with almost impossible deadlines. My friend and spouse Angela Yate for her research, production, and conscientious communications work throughout. And my friends and colleagues who served as the book's Brain Trust, and whose comments added another enriching dimension to the work.

DEDICATION

That you may learn to control your destiny
and get what you want out of life

Published by Adams Media, a division of F+W Media, Inc.
57 Littlefield Street, Avon, MA 02322. U.S.A.
www.adamsmedia.com

ISBN 10: 1-4405-3678-3
ISBN 13: 978-1-4405-3678-6

Printed in the United States of America.

10 9 8 7 6 5 4 3 2 1

This publication is designed to provide accurate and authoritative information with regard to the subject matter covered. It is sold with the understanding that the publisher is not engaged in rendering legal, accounting, or other professional advice. If legal advice or other expert assistance is required, the services of a competent professional person should be sought.

—From a *Declaration of Principles* jointly adopted by a Committee of the American Bar Association and a Committee of Publishers and Associations

Many of the designations used by manufacturers and sellers to distinguish their product are claimed as trademarks. Where those designations appear in this book and F+W Media was aware of a trademark claim, the designations have been printed with initial capital letters.

This book is available at quantity discounts for bulk purchases.
For information, please call 1-800-289-0963.

CONTENTS

CHAPTER 1
Wake Up, Stand Up, Lively Up Your Life 16

How business works, why jobs exist, and what this means for you.

CHAPTER 2
We Are All Professional Schizophrenics 27

We all develop a new, valid, and independent persona when we enter the professional world. Your dedication to the development of this professional self, and the transferable skills and professional values that underlie it, will determine the trajectory of your career.

CHAPTER 3
The Entry-Level Resume 50

Your resume is the most important financial document you will ever own. When it works, you do, and when it doesn't work, you don't either. Learn how to build a resume that impresses, even if you don't have any work experience.

CHAPTER 4

A successful job search depends on what you know and who you know. Learn how recruitment works and how to integrate networking into every job search strategy. Build deep, resilient, and relevant professional networks for your first job search and the subsequent strategic moves of a successful career.

CHAPTER 5

How to find and leverage internships and summer jobs, plus the best approaches to finding a professional job.

CHAPTER 6

How to integrate networking strategies into every aspect of job search and quadruple your interviews.

CHAPTER 7

Learn the preparation strategies that set the stage for turning job interviews into job offers.

CHAPTER 8

How interviewers organize interviews, how they think, why they do the things they do, and how to prepare.

INTRODUCTION

THIS IS YOUR LIFE

You didn't come to this book for a good time; you came because you need to take your first steps into the working world. You need to begin your professional career, get on the path to professional success, and start building a life of your own. *You came to this book today because there are things you want out of life and you want to learn what it will take to get them.*

Here are some little known facts about the world you face:

- You are at the beginning of what will likely be a fifty-year career.
- The statistics say you will probably change jobs (not always by choice) about every four years.
- You will probably have three or more distinct careers over the span of your professional life.

This means that job change is going to be a constant in your work life, and that even your *career* is likely to change—and more than once. No one is going to hand you a job, as those people in Admissions might have implied when they took your money.

You have to take responsibility and become the architect of your own success by learning what it takes to navigate the twists and turns of a long career, because if you don't take responsibility for your own success, nothing will happen. You'll get a first job and a year or two down the road you'll get another, but in seven years you'll begin to see only the backs and heels of people who were once your peers. At forty, you will see your career as just an ongoing series of jobs, and by fifty, when wage and age discrimination kicks in, you'll be lost and depressed because somehow it all passed you by and you have no idea where you went wrong.

Your parents grew up believing that hard work and loyalty would be rewarded with job security and steadily growing income, as it had been for generations. That was true once, but not any longer. Your parents' generations have been caught at a time of transition, from an era when career management meant nothing more than getting a job, working hard, and being loyal, to an era that Nobel prize–winning economist Paul Krugman describes as "an economy with no stability, no guarantees that hard work will provide a consistent living, and a constant possibility of being thrown aside simply because you happen to be in the wrong place at the wrong time."

You are entering the world of work at a time when every profession and every industry is going through upheaval as each adapts to the threats and opportunities offered by technology. But you can use this to your advantage. Yours is the first generation to grow up in a technology-driven world, and this will give you a distinct edge when you combine it with smart career-management strategies.

Your survival and success in life depend on your ability to guide the trajectory of your career. You probably don't know anything about career-management strategy, but after reading these last couple of paragraphs common sense tells you it's time to develop *the intelligent career-management strategies* that will help you get what you want out of life.

Your first step is to face the facts of professional life in the twenty-first century:

Change is constant; it is a given in your professional world. A successful career is no longer a given; it doesn't come as a gift with the purchase of your college diploma. The success of your career determines much that makes life worth living; it is a critical aspect of your life and it needs management if you hope to get what you want out of life.

While you must adapt to the realities of a professional world in which there is no job security and no assured path to success in return for hard work and loyalty, you also live in a world where there has never been more opportunity. When you adapt to the needs of an ever-changing professional landscape, you are perfectly positioned to seize the abundant opportunities that always accompany a changing of the eras. You grew up with change, and by continuing to adapt and evolve in tune with a world changing around you, you can recognize and seize opportunities that never existed before and to which most are still blind.

What should I be thinking about? Learning. First jobs aren't about pay, status, or title. Focus on how your first job will establish a solid foundation for where you want to be in ten years.

Carl Nielson, Principal, *www.careercoachingforstudents.net*

A Hard Lesson to Learn

In a world of constant change, your job-search and career-management skills are the most important skills you can ever develop. Few corporations have a sense of loyalty to employees; most only have loyalty to the shareholders, and the shareholders are only concerned with *profit—now*, this quarter. As an employee, you are simply a *small but important cog in the moneymaking machinery*, and if an employer can find a way to make money or save money by automating or exporting your job, giving it to someone cheaper, or making it part-time, then your life as you know it will disappear. That's the way things are, so cast off any mistaken notions of thick-and-thin fidelity to your employer and focus your attention with laser-like precision on what's best for *your* career and *your* life.

Know yourself. The more you understand yourself—your personality type, learning style, skills and interests, best environment, and values—and the more information you have, the better the choices you will make.

Allison Cheston, Career Connector, *www.allisoncheston.com*

Enlightened Self-Interest

When a company dispenses with your services, you are told that it's nothing personal—the company is doing what it must do to survive and satisfy the shareholders. To succeed in life, you need to do the same thing: You need to take control of your dreams, your economic survival, your success, and your destiny by acting with the same forethought, objectivity, and self-interest as a corporation.

Let's take that a step further: You need to become a corporation in mind, body, and spirit. Start thinking of yourself as a corporation that will always do what it must to survive—think of yourself as MeInc, a financial entity that must survive and prosper over the long haul. *You are MeInc*, a brand-new start-up with a successful future to be won.

As MeInc, the skills and experience you accumulate are the products and services you sell to employers and leverage in other ways. These product and services have to evolve over time to keep pace with and fulfill the needs of your customers, or the sale will go to a competitor.

This means that your corporation, MeInc, needs to get organized. You will need:

- *Research and Development:* to identify and develop products with the maximum marketplace appeal; in other words, you have to continually monitor market demands and develop the skills employers need.

> The person who commits himself or herself wholeheartedly to lifelong learning gets ahead and stays ahead.
>
> **Paul R. Bruno, PgMP, PMP,** Program Manager, *www.careertrend.com*

- *Marketing and Public Relations:* to establish credibility for the professional services you deliver, and to ensure that it becomes visible to an ever-widening circle, starting with your current department and expanding outward through the company, your local professional community, and beyond, as your strategic career plans dictate.

- *Sales:* to constantly develop new strategies to sell your products and services, including resume, job-search, interviewing, negotiation, and other career-management tools.
- *Strategic Planning:* to plan strategies for job security and growth within a company, time strategic career moves that take you to new employers, monitor the health of your profession, and make plans for career change; and all *on your timetable.* Working with R & D and Marketing, Strategic Planning will also constantly monitor opportunities and strategies for the pursuit of completely new revenue streams—alternate entrepreneurial endeavors that minimize disruption of MeInc's cash flow and maximize the odds of success for these endeavors.
- *Finance:* to ensure you invest wisely in initiatives that will deliver a Return On Investment (ROI). You must invest time, effort, and finances in your professional future to increase your odds of success.

You might think this advice is more for the guy with a mortgage and alimony payments, rather than someone like you who's just out of school and perhaps still living at home until he can get his foot in the door of the professional world; but you would be wrong.

You must start investing yourself in your future success now, rather than fritter away your income on the instant gratification drummed into your head by 24/7 media. This is important: You have been raised to be a good consumer and to live in debt. You probably spend eight hours a day in front of a screen—computer, television, tablet, smartphone—and absorb around 3,000 advertising messages a day. To make your dreams come true, you have to break free from this indoctrination and look to the horizon and where you want to be. You need to make a commitment now to invest yourself, your time, and your income in the activities that will make MeInc successful and give you the opportunity for a fulfilling life.

If the idea of starting your career off right with a businesslike approach makes sense, *Knock 'em Dead: Secrets & Strategies for First-Time Job Seekers* will give you the tools to make it happen. I've been at this for more than thirty years, and over this time, in fifteen books, countless articles, blogs, coaching session, webinars, and TV and radio appearances, I have evolved a practical, commonsense approach to achieving success in a changed and changing world. It's an approach that weaves cutting-edge job-search and career-management strategies into a revolutionary approach to getting what you want out of life.

This is what I think about every day, and what you are going to read has never been said before, unless you have seen this philosophy evolve over the sixty-eight editions of my fifteen books. *Knock 'em Dead: Secrets & Strategies for First-Time Job Seekers* brings all the diverse threads of my body of work together in a single narrative, giving you the *must-have* knowledge and tools to launch your career and build a life of professional success and personal fulfillment, as *you* define it.

Just as your ultimate career path may not be the one you initially choose, neither was mine; I didn't set out in life to become a career-management expert. My career and special expertise evolved out of a series of different jobs that gave me an unusually comprehensive understanding of the world of work, and these professional experiences combined with an ability to communicate, an inquiring mind, and a passion for helping others. I've been in the trenches as an international technology headhunter, a Director of HR for a publicly traded technology company, and a Director of Training and Development for a division of a *Fortune* 500 company, and in these capacities I have been at the table for countless hires, promotions, and terminations. The result is that over thirty-five years later I have lived through and thought through the issues of professional success more carefully than most.

We're going to talk all about the challenges you face coming to this first job search in a time of nearly unprecedented economic upheaval, but we're also going to talk about the rest of your professional life, because the time to worry about long-term career management is *now*, right at the beginning of your career. If you're willing to do the work, think about the long-term, and stick to the *Knock 'em Dead* plan, you will emerge from the ordeal of this first professional job search as a gainfully employed professional with a promising future in front of you—and with a concrete agenda that will make that promise a reality.

And along the way, I'll even show you how to integrate your entrepreneurial and creative dreams into your career-management strategy, so you can bring them to life too. Pay attention and this book could change the trajectory of your life forever.

—Martin Yate, CPC

THE KNOCK 'EM DEAD
BRAIN TRUST

Over the years I've met thousands of professionals in fields related to employment, and a select group of these people, whose work focuses on helping graduates like you get started in life, are going to join our conversation, enriching it throughout with pithy and helpful comments.

Their comments come from a questionnaire of seventy-plus questions, and often the short quotes you will see are part of a much longer commentary on that topic, from which I had to cull the essential nuggets of wisdom to make the page count allowed for the book. Choosing the quotes I use to enrich the conversation you and I are beginning was difficult because they had so much to say; and it occurred to me that you might like to see the full commentary of some or all of these career experts. So on the blog pages at *www.knock emdead.com* you'll find a tab for *Secrets & Strategies for First-Time Job Seekers*, and there you will be able to access the full wisdom of these experts. You can also find a directory of contact information for the *Secrets & Strategies Brain Trust* at the end of the book.

What you hold in your hands are the essentials for building a successful professional life, and you'll see my friends and colleagues adding to the conversation in very perceptive ways. If you want success, stability, freedom, and a meaningful, fulfilled life, I have a plan, and we're here to help.

PART I
WELCOME TO
THE PROFESSIONAL
WORLD

CHAPTER 1

WAKE UP, STAND UP, LIVELY UP YOUR LIFE

You came to this book because you're savvy enough to know that transitioning from school to work, and then navigating the twists and turns of a professional career, requires more than a hope and a prayer. You want to discover the practical strategies that will give you an edge over most of your peers, who haven't yet figured out the frat party's over. But awareness doesn't lessen your anxiety; you are only too aware that the first step of your career is one of the most important, and that the coming months should mark your successful crossing of the final bridge into adulthood. It's all up to you now.

Being nervous about this transition is a natural reaction to entering such a forbidding work world; after all, economists are saying that this is one of the most challenging times to start a career in modern history. Yet while many graduates from recent years still have not found professional jobs suitable to their education, this will not be your outcome: Your drive to succeed, coupled with the tools for career success you are about to learn, will ensure your success.

Even in an economy as bad as this one, there are plenty of jobs out there. Our economy is still the largest in the world, and throughout the last five years of recession not a month has gone by in which less than four million new jobs were posted on the Internet. Bottom line: there are plenty of great opportunities for the young professional willing to take the skills of career management seriously.

If you want to make a successful transition into the professional world, you have to get involved in managing the trajectory of your professional life. Successful careers don't just happen; they stem from an understanding of the business world and the application of integrated career-management strategies that will enable you to:

- Develop a resume that works
- Get job interviews with good companies
- Turn those interviews into offers
- Make a success of your first job
- Secure raises and promotions
- Plan and execute job and career changes on a timetable of your choosing
- Integrate and pursue entrepreneurial and dream careers

This is *your* life, and what you make of it is up to you, because no one else really gives a damn beyond your immediate family, and they can no longer be expected to support a full-grown adult. If you are intent on building a successful professional life and willing to learn and apply these job-search and career-management secrets and strategies, you will start your professional life off on the right track. I'll share all the tools you'll need to get that first job, make a success of it, win promotions, and change jobs and careers. These are secrets and strategies you will use successfully throughout your entire career, but the bottom line is that while I can show you what to do and how to do it, *it's your life, and what you make of it is up to you.*

How do I get my career off to a good start? Work your tail off so that you can move up the ladder to a leadership position that allows you to manage your own time.

Leslie Zaikis, Director of Business Development, *www.levoleague.com*

As you use the secrets and strategies in this book to execute a successful job search, turn interviews into offers, and get off on the right foot with your new job, you will also discover *a complete career-management strategy* for your career going forward. In these pages you will learn strategies not only for navigating the twists and turns of your professional career, but for giving your life real meaning, because you will discover how to successfully integrate both entrepreneurial endeavors and your dreams into a workable career-management plan designed for the modern world. I have inhabited this world throughout my professional life and I won't waste your time; so much as you can at this critical time in your life, relax, open your ears, and get on board with a commonsense plan for getting what you want out of your life.

Think about Your Goals

What do I want out of life? The more clearly you can envision life goals—including those dreams everyone told you not to waste your time with—and see a real path to achieving some of them, the more effort you will put into the work that has to be done today and every day along the path that brings them to reality. *Look at where you want to be ten or twenty years from now.* And those interests and dreams that give meaning to your life? Stop cramming them under the bed. Haul them out and reexamine them as you read and learn—you might find they don't belong there. Bring all these long-term goals and dreams into focus; own them, don't be scared by what others might think, and don't give up . . . ever.

This is not an either/or world anymore. Like many others, you've probably been told, "Find *one* thing you like, make it your career and settle down to it for a lifetime." But most of what you have been told doesn't make sense—life isn't that simple and you are too complex a being. I like to write; but all day, every day for fifty years? *Sweet baby Jesus, I'm ready, take me now.*

The reality is that you *can* and you *should* have multiple career goals and multiple career paths: for climbing the corporate ladder, for starting your own business, for writing that book or becoming a painter. Other people have made it happen, and you can too; in the following pages, as I share cutting-edge strategies for resumes, networking, job search, and turning interviews into job offers, I'll also gradually unfold the secrets and strategies you can use to bring those multiple, long-term career goals to life.

You might have dreams of career paths that seem impossible or that common sense tells you are hare-brained; yet all of them hold value and could well be achievable. Whatever those dreams might be, they are going to fall into one of three categories:

1. *Core career:* I'll show you how best to land that next job and how to make it as secure as it can possibly be, how to land the plum assignments and win raises and promotions, how to navigate strategic career moves within your industry, even how to decide on new career paths.
2. *Dream career:* Your dream might be to succeed as a writer, painter, singer in the band, or landscape gardener. I'll show you key strategies that can bring your dreams to life.
3. *Entrepreneurial career:* You'll learn how to seamlessly integrate plans for an entrepreneurial career into the pursuit of success in your *core career.* You'll recognize that they aren't mutually exclusive: They are attainable and can even be complementary.

We'll develop the means for achieving them throughout the book and bring them together in Chapter 15 when we discuss how to integrate the pursuit of *multiple parallel career paths* into jump-starting and pursuing success in your core career. But don't jump ahead: there's a plan, a methodology, and a new way of looking at your professional life that you need to soak up before it will all make sense.

Choose a Professional Core Career Wisely

As the MeInc philosophy unfolds, you will examine different paths to achieving a life that offers financial security and fulfillment, including becoming successful as an entrepreneur and in your dream career. With this approach, you aren't restricted to either/or career choices, but you *are* advised to pursue a professional *core career*. You need a roof over your head while you pursue your dreams, and just as important, a professional *core career* gives you the business experience that will increase your abilities to get your *entrepreneurial* and *dream careers* off the ground.

With all its lack of security, a traditional *core career* is still the most reliable route to economic wellbeing: living the American dream of having a home, a car, disposable income, perhaps raising a family and taking vacations. When you are making a career choice for the first time, you need to look at your options with a clear head. While there is no real job security in traditional career paths anymore, some professions, some industries, are much better bets than others.

Some people graduate and have no idea what they should do to make a living and a life. Some people know exactly what they want to do, and some of these people have known since they were snot-nosed kids. Other people can be happily guided by family tradition, while some cannot: I come from a family of doctors, surgeons, nurses, and health professionals but I faint at the sight of blood. The rest of us float indecisively in a sea of uncertainty.

> Your first job out of school might not be what you always dreamed of doing. No matter what situation you find yourself in, never think you are entitled to something else. Success and opportunity often come when you work to make good things happen.
>
> **Joshua Waldman,** Author, *Job Searching with Social Media for Dummies*, *www.careerenlightenment.com*

While *core career* choice should certainly take into account personal preferences, it should not be made in the belief that the career you choose will lead to lifelong security or that it will satisfy all your needs for today and always. Even people in the most secure of professions, doctors and lawyers for example, experience career problems that lead to career change. Nothing is certain in this life except change, and you need to learn how to manage the inevitable twists and turns of the long career ahead—because how you learn to navigate your career will dictate the degree of your long-term success and fulfillment.

Because of these considerations, *core career* choice should be based on pragmatism, and it can afford to be when a *core career* doesn't need to be the sum of your life, but part of a more intelligent approach to career management that embraces other options and supports your need for success, personal fulfillment, and financial security.

> Get serious about what you want out of life. Knowing what you want gives you direction, and makes it easier to get what you're after.
>
> **Josh Tolan**, CEO, *www.sparkhire.com*

Smart *core career* choice should take into account your skills, aptitudes, and preferences; your career services counselors have batteries of great tests you can take to help you learn about career choices that might work for you. These tests aren't oracles that dictate what you *must* do with your life, they are simply tools to help you think about options that might appeal to and make sense for you. Take advantage of these services as soon as you can, and if you have graduated but haven't bothered to take any career choice tests, go back to the career services department and take some now.

Having come up with a short list of career choices with the help of career tests, you should also consider:

- The projected health of the industry sectors you are considering
- The projected growth of the target job(s) you are considering
- The relative flexibility offered by that degree/job/industry combination in allowing you to change jobs and professions in the future

An industry sector/profession with healthy growth projections will deliver more job opportunities and better professional growth in good times and bad.

Within the profession/industry sector(s) under evaluation, you should consider the projected health of target jobs. Jobs with high projected growth potential—20-plus percent growth over the next decade is considered pretty healthy—are better than jobs with little or no projected growth.

The absolute number of people holding that job title today and on which the growth projections are based is also important: A projected 20 percent growth rate on a job that already has 3 million people holding that job title suggests greater security than a job with a projected 20 percent growth rate based on 35,000 people.

> **How do I get my career off to a good start?** Take it seriously. You've been working your whole life to get to "Go," and now you are here.
>
> **Lori Ruff,** CEO, *www.integratedalliances.com*

What Comes First, the Career Choice or the Degree?

Paying for college is expensive, so you want to make the smartest choices that also offer the greatest flexibility for changing jobs and careers later in your professional life.

1. Learn about the growth industries, the high-growth jobs within them, the academic credentials required for entry, and the credentials suggested for an accelerated start.
2. Cross-reference the academic requirements for the job(s) and career path(s) under consideration with the other jobs and careers people with these same degrees have pursued successfully.

This book does not address cross-referencing of career paths and degree programs. However, at *www.knockemdead.com* I have a database that houses information on *all major four-year degree programs,* the career directions that people successfully pursue with that degree, and some useful links with which to pursue your inquiries.

Based on this input, and having taken full advantage of any counseling and career choice/aptitude testing available to you, it will be possible to make practical *core career* choices based on opportunity for professional growth and job security.

Should You "Follow Your Bliss"?

A lot of career management advice to date tells you to find your passion, find your bliss, find something you love, and stick with it until you achieve success. This message gets lots of play because it tells people what they want to hear, but it is rarely practical, because coming out of school and crossing this last bridge into adulthood, your idea of bliss might not be a practical way to make a living. If you dream of being the bass player in a band, go ahead give it a shot, but at least do it in conjunction with a core career. If you are not prepared to compromise, whatever you do, don't stay too long at the party; entering the professional work force at the entry-level is tough enough up until twenty-five, but leave it two or three more years and employers begin to get really leery. Leave it too long and getting a foothold in a professional career can be very difficult. However, if you bear with me throughout this book, I will show you how to get what you want out of life: a pathway to a successful professional *core career* and a real shot at living your dreams.

The experts tell us to expect three or more careers over a work life, which, given a fifty-year work life, averages out to around fifteen years per career. Even if you become successful in one career, change happens and you may have to make a career change anyway.

Your needs/desires—the things you find worthwhile in life—will evolve as you age, and you will probably experience significant changes in these areas every seven to ten years. Because the metrics say that no job is secure and psychological research says that whatever rings bells for you today might not have the same relevance a few years down the road, career choice shouldn't necessarily be about finding your passion, although of course that's preferable if you can make a living doing things you enjoy.

Career Choice and the Bigger Picture

If you want to increase the likelihood of professional success, personal fulfillment, and financial independence, your *core career* is just that: central to your success, but not the only path to its achievement. You should pursue your *core career* with great energy and dedication for the rewards that success can bring, but your *core career* can also function as the training ground for your pursuit of parallel *dream* and *entrepreneurial careers*.

> **Build financial security,** become known and respected in your field, and develop separate sources of work that can provide additional streams of income. Build new skills and relationships, sustain networks, and work toward future opportunities. Plan and prepare for the day when you run your own business, eliminating dependency on an employer.
>
> **Marsha Connolly,** Managing Partner, *www.thenewrivergroup.com*

How Business Works

Most of your competitors for entry-level positions don't understand why jobs exist. They might not come right out and say it, but in the back of their minds there's a vague but comforting idea that companies exist in order to give them money. They just don't understand how business works.

Companies exist to make money as quickly, efficiently, and reliably as possible. Companies make money by selling a product or service, and they prosper by becoming better and more efficient at it.

When a company saves time, it saves money, and then has more time to make more money—this is called productivity.

If a company can make money without employees, it will do so, because that means more money for the owners. Unfortunately for the owners, a company requires a complex machinery to deliver those products and services that bring in revenue. Every job is a *small but important cog in a complex moneymaking machine*, and every cog has to mesh with other cogs. The cogs also have to be oiled (salary) and maintained (vacations, benefits). This all costs money; payroll and benefits are generally thought to account for by far the largest slice of a company's income. If a company can redesign the machinery to do without that cog (automation) or can find a cheaper cog (outsourcing that job to Mumbai), of course it is going to do so.

There are two reasons jobs exist. First, as I've said, every job is a *small but important cog in the corporation's complex moneymaking machine*. Second, the company hasn't been able to automate that job out of existence because in your area of technical expertise, problems arise.

Consequently, the company hires someone who has the *technical skills* to solve these problems when they occur and who knows the territory well enough to predict and prevent many of these problems from arising in the first place. It doesn't matter what your job title is: You are always hired to be a problem-solver with a specific area of expertise.

Think about the nuts and bolts of all the summer jobs you've held. Whatever the job, it always comes down to *anticipating, preventing, and solving problems*. This enables the company to make money for the owners as quickly, efficiently, and reliably as possible. School didn't work like this, but the professional world does.

Critical thinking or problem solving is one of a set of specific *transferable skills* and *professional values* that help successful professionals execute their responsibilities well, whatever the profession or challenge facing them. They didn't learn these particular skills in school, and neither did you. But when your future boss is looking to hire someone, her goal will be to find someone who *gets* how the business world works. Your *technical skills* may help get you an interview, but if you want to set off light bulbs in the interviewer's head and get that job, you must demonstrate that, unlike your peers, you know what it takes to help a company make money.

Start Toward Your Goals *Now*

You are at the beginning of your career and you'll find that a career is a marathon, not a sprint, so whatever your goals, the sooner you start toward them the better. Start imagining what you want your life to be like: not just this job search and that next job, but a detailed picture of what a fulfilling life would look like for you. Whatever your goals, the first step is a professional job that puts food on your table and a roof over your head; and with this you can begin to work steadily toward the realization of the career goals that will give your life meaning and fulfillment.

Calvin Coolidge once said, "The business of America is business." Business is at the heart of American prosperity. Even in times when unemployment has soared and banks have crumbled, across the country the wheels continue to turn, stuff continues to get made, and people continue to get jobs.

Even during an economic downturn—remember, they're cyclical and will occur regularly throughout your work life—*there are jobs.* But companies won't always show up on your doorstep, begging you to accept generous offers. You have to go out and win them.

CHAPTER 2

WE ARE ALL PROFESSIONAL SCHIZOPHRENICS

Over the years I've read a lot a lot of books about finding jobs, winning promotions, and managing your career. A few were insightful and many were innocuous, but one theme that runs through them all is plain harmful: Just be yourself.

"Who you are is fine. Just be yourself and everyone will love you." Wrong. If you've ever had a summer job or internship in an office, you'll probably have had the following experience. On your first day, when you summoned up the courage to go get your first cup of coffee, you found the coffee machine and there, stuck on the wall behind it, was a handwritten sign reading:

YOUR MOTHER DOESN'T WORK HERE
PICK UP AFTER YOURSELF

You thought, "Pick up after myself? Gee, that means I can't behave like I do at home or school and get away with it." And so you started to observe and emulate the more successful professionals around you. This is a crucial rite of passage for the professionals entering the workforce who intend to be successful. The lesson is that you need to learn how to behave in ways that encourage personal productivity and support a well-balanced professional workplace. What you have to do is develop a *professional persona* that enables you to survive and prosper in the professional world.

Some people are just better than the average bear at everything they do, and as a result they become more successful. It doesn't happen by accident; there is a specific set of *transferable skills* and *professional values* that underlies professional success: skills and values that employers all over the world in every industry and profession are anxious to find in candidates from the entry-level to the boardroom. It's not your fault that you didn't learn this in school, but it should have been part of your education, because these skills and values are the foundation of every successful career. They break down into these groups:

1. *Transferable Skills That Apply in All Professions.* These are the skills that underlie your ability to execute the *technical skills* of your job effectively, whatever that job may be; for example, *multitasking skills* are critical to success in every profession. These *transferable skills* are the foundation of any professional success you may have in this or any other career that you pursue over the years (including any *dream* and *entrepreneurial careers*).

2. *Professional Values.* The *professional values* are a set of beliefs that enable all professionals to make the right judgment calls during the working day to ensure that personal integrity and the best interests of the department and the employer are always served. They complement the *transferable skills* and together provide a firm foundation for a successful professional life.

> The transferable skills get you hired—period. People who can clearly state these skills in a resume and online profile get noticed. People who can articulate these skills in an interview have a distinct advantage over their competition.
>
> **Mark Babbitt,** CEO and Founder, *www.youtern.com*

A Review of Transferable Skills and Professional Values

As you read through the following breakdown of each *transferable skill* and *professional value* you may, for example, read about *communication*, and think, "Yes, I can see how communication skills are important in all jobs and at all levels of the promotional ladder, and, hallelujah, I have good communication skills." If this happens, take time to recall examples of your *communication skills* and the role they play in the success of your work.

You might also read about *multitasking skills* and realize that here is something that needs more work. Whenever you identify a *transferable skill* that needs work, you have found a *professional development project* that will repay your attention for the rest of your working life, no matter how you make a living.

> The work you do belongs to your employer, but the skills you build are yours to keep and can be applied in a lot of different situations; they'll truly help you achieve success.
>
> **Leslie Ayres,** Job Search Guru, *www.thejobsearchguru.com*

Here are the *transferable skills* and *professional values* that will not only help you stand out during this crucial first job search, but will also be an integral part of every aspect of your future success.

Transferable Skills	Professional Values
Technical	*Motivation and Energy*
Critical Thinking	*Commitment and Reliability*
Communication	*Determination*
Multitasking	*Pride and Integrity*
Creativity	*Productivity*
Teamwork	*Systems and Procedures*
Leadership	

Transferable Skills

Technical Skills

The *technical skills* of your profession are the foundation of all success; without them you won't even land a job, much less succeed in your career. *Technical skills* speak to your *ability* to do the job, those essentials necessary for success in the day-to-day execution of your duties. It means you know which skills and tools are needed for a particular task and possess the know-how to use them productively and efficiently. These *technical skills* vary from profession to profession and do not necessarily refer to anything technical *per se* or to technology skills.

However, it is a given that one of the *technical skills* essential to every job is technological adaptivity. You must be proficient in all computer and Internet-based applications relevant to your work. Even when you are not working in a technology field, strong *technology skills* will enhance stability and help you leverage professional growth.

When people are referred to as "professionals," it means they possess the appropriate *technical* and *technology skills* necessary for success in their profession and have interwoven them with the other major *transferable skills*. Staying current with the essential *technical* and *technology skills* of your chosen career path through ongoing professional education is going to be an integral part of your growth and stability. That's why the education section toward the end of your resume can be an important tool in developing your *professional brand*: It speaks to your technical competence and to your commitment, exemplified by your continuing pursuit of professional skills.

> Don't discount yourself as a job seeker if a position requires a degree that you haven't completed. Employers will take chances on employees who are on their way there but just haven't arrived yet.
>
> **Jessica Hernandez**, President, *www.greatresumesfast.com*

By 2015, 60 percent of the jobs available will require skills held by 20 percent of the population, according to a recent study by a recruitment metrics company.

Technology constantly changes the nature of our jobs and the ways in which they are executed. As a result, if you want to stay employable, you need stay current with the skills most prized in your professional world.

In addition to your job-specific *technical skills*, which you take from position to position within your current profession, there is also a body of skills that are just as desirable in other jobs and other professions as they are in yours. Possession of them will not only enhance your employability in your current profession, it will also ease your transition when you change careers: something that the statistics say you will do three or more times over the span of your work life. It will also help in your pursuit of entrepreneurial dreams.

Employers welcome employees who, in addition to the must-haves of the job, possess the written *communication skills* to write a PR piece or a training manual, who know how to structure and format a proposal, who are able to stand up and make presentations, or who know how to research, analyze, and assimilate hard-to-access data.

Some of the transferable *technical skills* sought across a wide spectrum of jobs include:

- Selling skills—Even in non-sales jobs, the art of persuasive communication is always appreciated, because no matter what the job . . . you are always selling something to someone.
- Project management skills
- Six Sigma skills
- Lean Management skills
- Quantitative analysis skills
- Theory development and conceptual thinking skills
- Counseling and mentoring skills
- Writing skills for PR, technical, or training needs
- Customer Resource Management (CRM) skills
- Research skills
- Social networking skills

There are also technology skills that have application within all professions in our technology-driven world. It is pretty much a given that you need to be computer literate to hold down any job today—just about every job expects competency with MS Word and e-mail. Similarly, Excel or PowerPoint are becoming skills it is risky not to possess.

Any employer is going to welcome a staff member who knows his way around spreadsheets and databases, who can update a webpage, or who is knowledgeable in CRM.

Some of the technology skills that enhance employability on non-technology jobs include:

- Database
- Spreadsheet
- Documents
- Presentations
- Communications

Eventually more and more of these skills will become specific requirements of the jobs of the future, but when you possess them before that time comes, possession of transferable *technical skills* adds a special sauce to your candidacy for any job.

You can find useful links for professional development at:

www.knockemdead.com
www.mindtools.com/pages/main/newMN_ISS.htm
www.mindtools.com/page8.html

Communication Skills

Without *communication* you live in silence and isolation; with *communication* you make things happen in your life.

In our knowledge-economy, how you think and how you communicate those thoughts is your most valuable asset. Most professional jobs require that you make informed decisions, and you will need to be able to justify those decisions.

Joshua Waldman, Author, *Job Searching with Social Media for Dummies*, *www.careerenlightenment.com*

As George Bernard Shaw said, "The greatest problem in communication is the illusion that it has been accomplished." Every professional job today requires *communication skills*; promotions and professional success are impossible without them. Good verbal *communication skills* enable you to accurately process incoming information and also to present outgoing information persuasively and appropriately to your audience and message, so that it is understood and accepted.

But *communication* embraces much more than listening and speaking. When the professional world talks about *communication skills*, it is referring to four primary skills and four supportive skills.

The primary *communication skills* are:

- Verbal skills—what you say and how you say it.
- Listening skills—listening to understand, rather than just waiting your turn to talk.
- Writing skills—clear written communication, essential for any professional career. It creates a lasting impression of who you are.
- Technology communication skills—the way you communicate and your ability to navigate the new communication media.

The four supportive *communication skills* are subtler, but nevertheless they impact every interaction you have with others. They are:

- Grooming and dress—they tell others who you are and how you feel about yourself.
- Social graces—these are demonstrated by how you behave around others. If your table manners are sketchy, odds are you'll never sit

at the chairman's table or represent your organization at the higher levels.

- Body language—this displays how you're feeling deep inside, a form of communication that predates speech. For truly effective communication, what your mouth says must be in harmony with what your body says.
- Emotional IQ—your emotional maturity in dealing with other adults in professional settings.

> Like it or not, the responsibility of translating what you can DO into language employers can understand is totally yours.
>
> **Dr. Kate Duttro,** Career Coach for Academics, *www.careerchangeforacademics.com*

Develop effective *communication skills* in all these areas and you'll gain enormous control over what you can achieve, how you are perceived, and what happens in your life.

You can check out resources for developing each of these skills at: *www.knockemdead.com.*

- Verbal Skills
  www.wordsmith.org/awad/index.html
  www.mindtools.com/page8.html
- Listening Skills
  www.mindtools.com/CommSkll/ActiveListening.htm
- Writing skills
  www.mindtools.com/CommSkll/WritingSkills.htm
- Body Language
  *www.helpguide.org/mental/eq6_nonverbal_communication
  .htm#improving*
- Social Graces
  http://windowscollective.net/social_graces.html
- Dress and Grooming
  www.tips.learnhub.com/lesson/2800-tips-on-business-dress-etiquette-and-grooming (guys, remember to scroll down)

- Emotional Intelligence
  www.psychology.about.com/lr/emotional_intelligence/337325/1/

Critical Thinking Skills

You know to come in from the rain, right? Then you know *critical thinking* impacts everything you do in life.

Life and the world of work are full of opportunity, and every one of those opportunities is peppered with problems. With *critical thinking skills* you can turn those opportunities into achievement, earnings, and fulfillment. This is the professional-world application of all those *problem-solving skills* you've been developing since grade school: a systematic approach to uncovering all the issues related to a particular challenge.

Critical thinking, analytical, or problem-solving skills allow the successful professional to logically think through and clearly define a challenge and its desired solutions, and then evaluate and implement the best solution for that challenge from all available options.

> Communication, critical thinking/problem solving, and multitasking (time management and organization) are skills you need to succeed. If you don't have them, you will most likely remain unemployed. Robots will eventually be able to do everything you are qualified for.
>
> **Scott Keenan**, HR Generalist, *www.educatedandinexperienced.blogspot.com*

You examine the problem and ask the critical questions:

- What's the problem?
- Who is it a problem for?
- Why is it a problem?
- What is causing this problem?
- What are the options for a solution?
- What problems might a given solution create?
- What is the most suitable solution?

You look through the factors affecting each possible solution and decide which solutions to keep and which to disregard. Once you have decided on a course of action, you plan out the steps, the timing, and the resources to make it happen.

- How long will it take to implement this solution?
- How much will it cost?
- What resources will I need?
- Can I get these resources?
- Will the solution really resolve the problem to everyone's benefit?
- Will this solution cause its own problems?

> Employers favor candidates with exceptional analytical skills and business acumen. You can demonstrate these qualities in terms of stuff you did at school: tracking, analyzing, interpreting, and reporting data. However, the real "attraction" is to candidates who combine these skills with superior interpersonal skills.
>
> **Sean Koppelman**, President, *www.thetalentmagnet.com*

Einstein said that if he had one hour to save the world he would spend fifty-five minutes defining the problem. It's a thought worth remembering, because a properly defined problem always leads to a better solution, and 50 percent of the success of any project is in the prep. *Critical thinking* is an integral part of preparation.

Check out this link to learn more about developing your *critical thinking skills*:

www.litemind.com/problem-definition/

> Transferable skills are essential to getting a job, keeping the job, and getting promotions. Those with strong communication and problem-solving skills are going to be the people coworkers go to with problems and concerns.
>
> **Josh Tolan**, CEO, *www.sparkhire.com*

Multitasking

Multitasking is the ability to maintain a timely delivery schedule for a constantly changing roster of parallel projects. This is one of the most frequently used words in job postings and therefore one of the most sought-after skills of the new world of work. Yet most people don't understand what multitasking entails. According to numerous studies, the *multitasking* demands of modern professional life are causing massive frustration and emotional trauma for professionals everywhere. However, the problem is *not multitasking*, the problem is the assumption that *multitasking* means being reactive to *all* incoming stimuli and therefore jumping around from one task to another as the emergency of the moment dictates. Such a definition of *multitasking* would of course leave you feeling as if wild horses were attached to your extremities and tearing you limb from limb.

> A successful professional is, amongst other things, someone who can effectively manage multiple projects and deadlines, and who knows how to prioritize and effectively communicate re-prioritization when necessary.
>
> **Chris Perry**, Brand and Marketing Generator, *www.careerrocketeer.com*

Few people understand that multitasking is *not* being continually distracted by the latest incoming stimuli; instead, *multitasking* skills are built on sound *time-management and organizational* abilities. Here are the basics to help you understand, execute, and talk intelligently about your *multitasking* capabilities:

Establish Priorities

Multitasking is based on three things:

1. Establishing priority activities for your day
2. Building a plan based on your established priorities
3. Sticking to your plan and managing your time based on the priorities itemized in your plan

Plan your work and work your plan. Those who are better prepared and plan better will get ahead in the long run. Never rely on luck; your career goal should never be to win the lottery.

Marshall J. Karp, MA, NCC, LPC, Career Counselor, *www.marshalljkarp.com*

The Plan, Do, Review Cycle

At the end of every day you review:

- What happened: A.M. and P.M.?
- What went well? Do more of it.
- What went wrong? How do I fix it? Where can I get advice?
- What priorities do I need to put on tomorrow's plan?
- Rank each priority: A = Must be completed tomorrow. B = Good to be completed tomorrow. C = If there is spare time from A and B priorities.
- Make a prioritized To-Do list.
- Come to work the next day and execute your plan, unless management gives you a new "A" priority.

Doing this at the end of the day keeps you informed about what you have achieved, and lets you know that you have invested your time in the most important activities today and will do the same tomorrow, so you feel better, sleep better, and come into the office in the morning focused and ready to be productive.

Time-management and organization are essential. Organize your goals in writing so that you have a clear plan of action to get the job done!

Jacqui Barrett-Poindexter, MRW, CEIP, Partner and Chief Career Writer, *www.careertrend.net*

With *multitasking* (time management and organization) *skills* you can bring your dreams to life. Without them, you will forever spin in underachieving circles. There are two types of people in the world: the task-oriented, who let tasks expand to fill all the time allotted to them, and the goal-oriented, who organize, prioritize, and strive to get all work completed in an orderly manner as quickly and efficiently as quality will allow. Sometimes the only difference between these two types is that one group learned how to *multitask*. You get one guess as to who has the most successful and fulfilled life. The ability to *multitask* increases productivity; this ability is based on the sensible expediency of ordering your activities based on their priorities and the time of day, and the consistently efficient use of every moment of your time. The people who do this—often characterized as high achievers and goal-oriented because they get so much done—are just people who have learned how to organize themselves and consequently work with more purpose. The result is that they can *multitask* and seriously outperform their peers.

Teamwork

Most students come out of college already thinking about joining the ranks of management. It's okay to have this as your goal, but you need to understand what it takes to get there. To become a successful leader you need to understand how and why teams work well and what makes teams falter; to break into management and become a successful leader, you first have to become a successful *team player*.

Companies are in the business of generating uninterrupted revenue streams. Usually, the bigger the revenue stream, the more complexities are involved in maintaining and growing that revenue stream. At the same time, greater complexity invariably requires more and bigger teams to master those complexities, and the members of these teams have to work together harmoniously for greatest productivity. Translation: If you are going to succeed in the professional world, you have to get along with others, and you have to consistently put the good of the team before your personal preferences.

> You need people to like and respect you in order to succeed. Not understanding how to build relationships will doom a career.
>
> **Leslie Ayres**, Job Search Guru, *www.thejobsearchguru.com*

Practically speaking, this means that you must work efficiently and respectfully with other people who have totally different responsibilities, backgrounds, objectives, and areas of expertise. It's true that individual initiative is important, but as a professional, much of the really important work you do will be done as a member of a group. Your long-term stability and success require that you learn the arts of cooperation, team-based decision-making, and team communication.

This is especially important if you dream of climbing the corporate ranks into a leadership position or having your own business one day, because before you can lead, you first have to learn how to follow. There's a reason people come up through the ranks rather than starting at the top, and it's not just about "proving yourself"—though it's about that too. Success at the top is built on a patient apprenticeship in the lower ranks, because good management relies on an intimate knowledge of how a business works from the ground up.

Teamwork demands that a commitment to the team and its success comes first. This means you take on a task because it needs to be done, not because it makes you look good.

As a team player you:

- Always cooperate.
- Always make decisions based on team goals.
- Always keep team members informed.
- Always keep commitments.
- Always share credit, never blame.

If you become a successful leader in your professional life, it's a given that you were first a reliable team player, because a leader must understand the dynamics of teamwork before she can leverage them.

When teamwork is coupled with the other *transferable skills* and *professional values, it results in greater responsibility and promotions.*

> Successful professionals collaborate well with others and are a pleasure to work with. They work hard, work smart, and get results.
>
> **Rich Grant,** Director of Career Services, *www.thomas.edu*

The Complex Transferable Skills

Each of the *transferable skills* helps you become successful in whatever career you pursue, because they help you do whatever you do well. At the same time, *transferable skills* rarely exist in a vacuum. Each interacts with one or more of the others as a given situation demands: For example, *communication skills* include listening skills, listening implies the goal of understanding, and understanding requires the use of your *critical thinking skills*.

There are seven *transferable skills*, and the sixth and seventh, *creativity* and *leadership*, are called *complex transferable skills* because they can only come into being when a fully integrated combination of each and every one of the other *transferable skills* is brought into play.

Creativity
There's a difference between *creativity* and just having ideas. Ideas are like headaches: We all get them once in a while, and like headaches they disappear as mysteriously as they arrived. *Creativity*, on the other hand, is the ability to develop those ideas with the strategic and tactical know-how that brings them to life. Someone is seen as creative when her ideas produce tangible results.

Creativity in your professional world will come from the frame of reference you will develop for your work, profession, and industry. As your skills develop and you achieve greater competency in all areas of your work, you will begin to see the *patterns* that lie behind everything you do. As you see these patterns of cause and effect with the daily challenges of your job, you will also begin to see solutions to those challenges that others might miss.

Creativity also demands that you harness other *transferable skills* to bring your ideas to life. *Creativity* springs from:

- Your *critical thinking skills*, applied within an area of *technical expertise* (an area where your *technical skills* give you a frame of reference for what works and what doesn't).
- Your *multitasking skills*, which in combination with your *critical thinking* and *technical skills* allow you to break your challenge down into specific steps and determine which approach is best.
- Your *communication skills*, which allow you to explain your approach and its building blocks persuasively to your target audience.
- Your *teamwork* and *leadership skills*, which enable you to enlist others and bring the idea to fruition.

Creative approaches to challenges can take time or can come fully formed in a flash, but the longer you work on developing the supporting skills that bring *creativity* to life, the more often they *will* come fully formed and in a flash.

> **Transferable skills.** The hiring managers I have worked with are diligent in screening for these skill sets.
>
> **Denise Wilkerson, RN, CPC,** Director of Executive Search,
> *www.globaledgerecruiting.com*

Here are five rules for building creativity skills in your professional life:

1. **Whatever you do in life, engage in it fully.** Commit to developing competence in everything you do, because the wider your frame of reference for the world around you, the more you will see the patterns and connectivity in your professional

world, and this breadth of knowledge will deliver the higher-octane fuel you need to propel your ideas to acceptance and reality.

2. **Learn something new every day.** Just because you're not going to class anymore doesn't mean it's time to stop learning. Treat the pursuit of knowledge as a way of life; absorb as much as you can about everything. Information exercises your brain, filling your mind with information and contributing to that ever-widening frame of reference that allows you to see those patterns behind a specific challenge. The result is that you will make connections others don't, and develop solutions that are seen as magically creative.

3. **Catch ideas as they occur.** Note them in your PDA or on a scrap of paper. Anything will do so long as long as you capture the idea.

4. **Welcome restrictions in your world.** They make you think, they test the limits of your skills and the depth of your frame of reference; they truly encourage *creativity*. Ask any successful business leader, entrepreneur, writer, artist, or musician.

   Restrictions in time, money, or resources are all negative in initial impact, but they become the realities under which you must operate. Consequently, the professional defines those restrictions very carefully and then proceeds with the work under these new guidelines. From a production POV (and creativity is all about giving abstract ideas some concrete form), restrictions make you think harder about the essentials and building blocks of your task. When you can take complex ideas and reduce them to their elemental parts, you have a real understanding of that task. Similarly, restrictions increase the need for simplicity in design, function, and expression, and simplicity always leads to elegance no matter the project at hand. Restrictions are part of life; you can whine or suck it up and get on with the job.

5. **Don't spend your life glued to Facebook or TV.** You need to live life, not watch it go by out of the corner of your eye. If you do watch television, try to learn something or motivate

yourself with science, history, or biography programming. If you surf the Internet, do it with purpose.

Building *creativity skills* enables you to bring your ideas to life, and the development of each of these seven interconnected *transferable skills* will help you bring your dreams to life too.

Leadership Skills

"A leader has two important characteristics; first, he is going somewhere; second, he is able to persuade other people to go with him." The guy who said this, Maximilien Robespierre, was a principal figure in the French Revolution and literally changed the world. As you develop *teamwork* skills—which is a must if you ever hope to lead—notice how you are willing to follow true leaders and how you don't fall in line with people who don't respect you and who don't have your best interests at heart.

When you are credible, when people believe in your competence and believe you have everyone's success as your goal, those people will follow you; *you* accept responsibility, but "we" gets the credit. When your actions inspire others to think more, learn more, do more, and become more, you are on your way to becoming a leader.

Leadership is the most complex of all the *transferable skills* that you will develop to make a success of your professional work life. It is a combination and outgrowth of all the other *transferable skills*.

- Your job as a leader is to help your team succeed, and your *teamwork skills* give you the smarts to pull a team together as a cohesive unit.
- Your *technical* expertise, *critical thinking*, and *creativity skills* help you correctly define the challenges your team faces, and give you the wisdom to guide your reports toward the thinking that delivers the appropriate solutions.
- Your *communication skills* enable your team to *buy into* your directives and goals. There's nothing more demoralizing than a leader who can't clearly articulate why you're doing what you're doing.

- Your consummate *technical skills* combined with the consistent application of all the other *transferable skills* in your work will give you an ever-widening frame of reference for the challenges your job delivers every day. This ability to look at challenges from many different viewpoints and make connections that others with a more restricted POV will miss is creativity at work.
- Your *multitasking skills*, based on sound *time management* and *organizational* abilities, enable you to create a practical blueprint for success, and enable your team to take ownership of the task and deliver the expected results on time.

Leadership is a combination and outgrowth of all the *transferable skills* plus the clear presence of all the *professional values* we are about to discuss. Leaders aren't born, they are self-made. And just like anything else, becoming one takes hard work.

For advice on how to further develop this skill check out the following link:

www.mindtools.com/pages/main/newMN_LDR.htm

Professional Values

Professional values are an interconnected set of core beliefs that enable professionals to determine the right judgment call in any situation. Highly prized by employers, this value system also complements and is integral to the *transferable skills*.

Professional Values. These are the basic building blocks of professional success. At the start of your career everybody is equally talented, so you must set yourself apart as someone who has a strong work ethic, an ability to play on a team, and a genuine enthusiasm for the job.

Caroline Dowd-Higgins, Career Director, Maurer School of Law; CBS Radio Host, *www.carolinedowdhiggins.com*

Motivation and Energy

Motivation and *energy* express themselves in your engagement with and enthusiasm for your work and profession. They involve an eagerness to learn and grow professionally, and a willingness to take the rough with the smooth in pursuit of meaningful goals. *Motivation* is invariably expressed by the *energy* you demonstrate in your work. You always give that extra effort to get the job done and get it done right.

Commitment and Reliability

This means dedication to your profession, and the empowerment that comes from knowing how your part contributes to the whole. Your *commitment* expresses itself in your *reliability*. The *committed* professional is willing to do whatever it takes to get a job done, whenever and for however long it takes to get the job done, even if that includes duties that might not appear in a job description and that might be perceived by less enlightened colleagues as beneath them.

Reliability is a major issue for new graduates. You can no longer roll out of bed at noon and shuffle into class wearing yesterday's clothes. Because employers are apprehensive about the reliability of young candidates, you can set yourself apart by taking extra care to incorporate this *professional value* into your *professional persona*.

Determination

This, too, is a value that many young professionals have not yet developed, and that you can use to set yourself apart. The *determination* you display with both the tougher and the more boring aspects of your work speaks of a resilient professional who does not back off from less glamorous responsibilities or when a problem or situation gets tough. It's a *professional value* that marks you as someone who chooses to be part of the solution.

The *determined* professional has decided to make a difference with her presence every day, because it is the *right* thing to do, and because it makes the time go faster. She is willing to do whatever it takes to get a job done, and she will demonstrate that determination on behalf of colleagues who share the same values.

Pride and Integrity

Pride in yourself as a professional means always making sure the job is done to the best of your ability; this in turn means paying attention to the details and to the time and cost constraints. *Integrity* means taking responsibility for your actions, both good and bad, and it also means treating others, within and outside of the company, with respect at all times and in all situations. With *pride* in yourself as a professional with *integrity*, your actions will always be in the ethical best interests of the company, and your decisions will never be based on whim or personal preference.

> The more you act in alignment with professional values the clearer your direction and your sense of purpose will become. People will sense your integrity and trust you.
>
> **Phyllis Mufson**, Career Coach, *www.phyllismufson.com*

Productivity

You are always working toward *productivity* in your areas of responsibility, through efficiencies of time, resources, money, and effort.

Economy

Remember the word "frugal"? It doesn't mean poverty or shortages. It means making the most of what you've got, using everything with the greatest efficiency. Companies that know how to be frugal with their resources will prosper in good times and bad, and if you know how to be frugal, you'll do the same.

Systems and Procedures

This is a natural outgrowth of all the other *transferable skills* and *professional values*. Your *commitment* to your new profession in all these ways gives you an appreciation of the need for *systems* and *procedures* that a company only implements after careful thought.

Young professionals are the people most likely to buck the system and try to do things their own way; this invariably causes disruption and problems with management and coworkers, and often leads to disciplinary action. Your precocious understanding and respect for an employer's *systems and procedures* will go a long way toward getting off on the right foot in a new job.

You will take time to understand and always follow the chain of command. You are not the kind of troublemaker who implements "improved" procedures or encourages others to do so. If ways of doing things don't make sense or are interfering with efficiency and profitability, you work through the *system* to get them changed.

Developing mastery of the *transferable skills* and *professional values* supports your *enlightened self-interest*, because it will be repaid with job security and the promise of *professional development*. The more you are engaged in your new career, the more likely you are to join the inner circles that exist in every department and company, and that's where the plum assignments, raises, and promotions live.

Your Professional Brand

You have doubtless heard the term "branding" as a way of differentiating yourself from your professional peers in the eyes of the people who can advance your career: recruiters, hiring managers, and other superiors. Despite anything you may have heard to the contrary, a professional brand is not something you can create overnight. It takes time to develop and will evolve and change over a lifetime. At the beginning of your career, when you have no experience or any idea of what the *Inner Circle* looks for in a *professional brand*, creating one is difficult.

However, the *transferable skills* and *professional values* are the core of a desirable *professional brand* at even the highest ranks. Professionals who are seen to possess these skills become known and respected as consummate professionals.

Transferable skills are the active components of your ability to work independently. If you're early in your career, this is a cornerstone of the skill-set you need to demonstrate if you want to be given more autonomy, responsibility, and exposure to greater experiences.

Kevin Kermes, Founder, *www.careerattraction.com*

That you have these admirable traits is one thing; that *I* know you have them, well, that's another matter. These skills must become a part of you, and as you develop them and integrate them into your work every day, they will begin to define a desirable *professional brand* for you. You need to:

- Develop these *skills* and *values* in everything you do professionally.
- Make them a living dimension of your professional persona.
- When relevant and appropriate, reference them subtly in your resume and other written communications.
- Reference them appropriately in interviews as the underlying skills that will enable you to succeed in your chosen field.

RESOURCES You'll find these *transferable skills* and *professional values* referenced in all *Knock 'em Dead* books, but especially in the latest edition of *Knock 'em Dead: The Ultimate Job Search Guide.*

CHAPTER 3

THE ENTRY-LEVEL RESUME

Your resume is the most important financial document you will ever own. It demands your undivided attention, because when it works, the doors of opportunity open for you, but when it doesn't work, you don't either.

Do I Even Need a Resume?

You may been told that resumes are old-fashioned and that all you need now is a social media profile. At a minimum, you may be skeptical about the usefulness of a resume in today's high-tech work world. If so, I've got some bad news. A world without resumes is the sort of thing John Lennon sang about in "Imagine"—but it isn't going to happen.

An intelligently diversified approach to job search will take full advantage of the benefits of a strong social media presence (see Chapters 4–6), but your Facebook or LinkedIn page does a different job and does not replace your resume. In fact, your resume will form the foundation for leveraging social media.

Your resume comes first and your social media presence is subsequently built upon it. If you check out the websites of the people who write social media profiles, notice that they all require a copy of your resume to start the process. Your resume is the basis of an online social media profile.

Your Resume and Database Visibility

Resumes no longer go directly to someone's desk for review; they disappear into a database with millions of other resumes, and these databases can contain more than 35 million resumes. This means that making your resume visible to recruiters is a big challenge.

For anyone to actually review your resume, it will first have to be retrieved from the depths of the database by a recruiter using exactly the same tactics you would use to execute a Google search.

What's Important in a Resume

Titles Are Important

Every product ever sold has a name ("Coke") or a title (*Avatar*), because that's what draws the reader/viewer/buyer in. Every product in the world struggling for attention amidst the 3,000-plus advertising images that bombard us every day has a name/title as its first-line differentiator. A resume without a title will get about as many viewers as a movie without a title.

> I consider a resume visually first. I look for education, position titles, and companies. If I see things that I need, then I will read the resume.
>
> **Jim Rohan**, Senior Partner, J.P. Canon Associates

Keywords Are Important

> Keywords specific to your industry are absolutely critical if you want your resume to show up in database searches.
>
> **Marjean Bean, CPC**, President, MedIT Staff

Along with a job title, recruiters will search resume databases and social networking sites using terms relevant to the position they are trying to fill. Referred to as keywords, these words and phrases are pulled from the company's Job Description, a formal document that details exactly what the company is looking for.

The job postings you see online very often reflect the exact wording of the formal company job description that was developed to define the job. So you can look at a job posting and say to yourself, "This is how the employer prioritizes the job's needs, and these are the words she uses to express them." You can use this knowledge in writing your resume, in communication with corporate recruiters, and at job interviews.

But the first and most important place to employ this knowledge is in writing your resume. When a recruiter is searching a resume database, she first types a job title into a dialogue box, and then other dialogue boxes pop up and prompt her to type in the keywords and phrases that best capture the essence of that job. The keywords she will use are the ones from the company's internal Job Description. The resumes that perform best in these situations are the ones that use the same words the recruiters use: the words from the Job Description and Job Posting.

Once programmed to search for a specific set of words, the software scours the database and builds a list of all the resumes (or profiles, in the case of social networking sites) that contain *any* of the chosen keywords. It then weights the list. Those resumes with *the most frequent use and greatest number of keywords* rise to the top of the list. Preference in the weighting system is given to words that come near the top of the page. Because *recruiters very rarely go beyond the top twenty resumes in a database search*, not enough relevant keywords or keywords in the right place means no human eyes will review it.

If and when your resume reaches human eyes, the process is equally alarming. Recruiters will read resumes pulled from the database once, perhaps twice. The first reading is a skim that takes five seconds to a minute. The layout, font, font size, and overall visual accessibility of your resume are major factors in your presentation of yourself to recruiters. So no job title, no focus, and/or a lack of relevant, readily visible keywords likely means no second read. Your resume needs a relevant target job title that is focused on the target job's deliverables and contains keywords relevant to the execution of that job's responsibilities.

> Resumes should tell a compelling story about what you can do. The biggest mistake we see is a list of what you did at a job versus telling the story of how your combined work experiences will enable you to do the next job well.
>
> **Mark Babbitt**, CEO and Founder, *www.youtern.com*

Given these considerations, the next read is more careful. Recruiters look to see if the resume's claims hang together and tell the story of someone who really *gets* the job. Recruiters and HR typically start with up to twenty resumes and prune it to a *long list* of six to eight candidates who will be interviewed in some depth, and who, if they don't self-destruct, will have their resumes passed on to a hiring manager. The manager then determines the *short list* of candidates he will interview face-to-face.

Managers hate reading resumes; they just want to hire someone and get back to work. Bear this in mind, because you will use the insight to great advantage in your resume and in preparing for job interviews.

Even when your resume finally gets in front of human eyes, it has precious little time to make a convincing argument and lead to a telephone conversation. *The success of your entire job search depends on getting into conversation as quickly and as often as possible with people in a position to hire you.* Your resume plays a major role in this process, and it has to be up to the task. Fortunately, I have a way to make this happen.

The Solution: Target Job Deconstruction

Target Job Deconstruction (TJD) helps you understand how your potential employers (your customers) think about and express their needs for the job. This enables you to create a resume that speaks directly to their stated needs; a resume that:

- Establishes an achievable goal for your search
- Provides a template for the story your resume *must* tell to be successful
- Opens the door for interviews
- Prepares you for the questions interviewers will ask and helps you craft your answers
- If you have any work experience, can deliver examples with which to illustrate your answers

Draw on your leadership experience. Use numbers to show the budgets you oversaw or the number of people you managed as a student leader. Think about what you've done outside a work environment as though it were a work environment, and be specific. It's all about how you explain that experience in the context of business.

Amanda Pouchot, Founder, *www.levoleague.com*

How to Deconstruct Your Target Job

Your resume will obviously be most effective when it starts with a clear focus and understanding of a specific target job. *TJD* allows you to analyze exactly how employers prioritize their needs for your target job and the words they use to express those needs. With the insights you gain from Target Job Deconstruction, you will know exactly the story your resume needs to tell to sell your skills most effectively.

Since you are starting out you probably don't have much of a work history to dig into, but your competition doesn't either, and you can often use those part-time burger-flipping jobs to demonstrate your possession of the *transferable skills* and *professional values*.

The next few years will pass quickly and before you know it, the time will come to make your first professional job change. At this point you will be able to do *TJD* on the target job of your choice and look back into your work history for the skills and experiences that best demonstrate your qualifications for that job.

Step #1: Decide on a Primary Target Job

No employer is looking to give you or anyone else a start in life; she just has a position that needs to be filled by someone with the skills and interest to do the work. A resume that speaks directly to the needs of a specific type of job, using the words employers use in job postings, will always be more successful in getting you interviews than a general resume written without a target job focus.

> We've all heard real estate moguls say the way to success is "Location, location, location!" For resumes (and careers), the analogous advice is, "Focus, focus, focus!"
>
> **Dr. Kate Duttro,** Career Coach for Academics, *www.careerchangeforacademics.com*

Giving your resume target job focus means it is more likely to be found by recruiters in resume database searches, and more likely to resonate with those recruiters and hiring managers when they actually get to read it.

So of all the jobs you could do, decide on the one that you have both the credentials and the desire for: When you decide on an entry-level target job for which you have both the education and desire, it becomes an easier sell for you and an easier buy for the employer. You can then create your *primary* resume with a specific target job in mind.

By choosing the target job that you feel offers you the greatest chances of success, you will be able to build a stronger resume, and this will help propel your job search to success. This does not mean you cannot pursue any of those other jobs for which you have the education and desire. It means that if the job is worth pursuing, it is worth pursuing with a custom resume.

CREATING JOB-TARGETED RESUMES FOR THOSE *OTHER* *JOBS* YOU CAN DO

Once you have a *primary* resume tailored to the most logical focus for your job search, you can quite easily customize it for any other jobs that interest you. Invariably there is overlap in the skills and experience demanded by the different jobs, because in many instances they will be related. Consequently, you can take that primary resume, make a copy, re-title it, and, having completed the *TJD* sequence on the additional target job, make the necessary changes to give this additional resume the specific focus it needs to be found by recruiters in their database searches. You won't have to start from scratch, and you'll have a customized resume for each opportunity you want to pursue.

Step #2: Understanding Your Target Job

Collect a half-dozen job postings for your primary target job. To help you do this quickly, use one of the job posting aggregators like *www.SimplyHired.com* or *www.Indeed.com*. Each of them will search thousands of job sites for you. These job aggregators or job spiders all work similarly—the home page has a couple of dialogue boxes: one for a job title and one for a geographic area. If you cannot find half a dozen jobs in your target location, just try another major metropolitan area. For the purpose of *TJD* it doesn't matter where the jobs are located: You are just trying to get inside the collective head of your customers to understand exactly what they want to buy and how you can best package yourself to suit their needs. You do this by learning how they prioritize their needs for this job and the words they use to express those needs.

Put the job postings you find in a folder on your desktop. From these six job postings (or more: the larger your sample, the better) you will discover how employers think about, prioritize, and express their needs when writing job descriptions and hiring. The result will be a template that describes your target job *the way employers themselves think about and describe it.*

Step #3: Look at Your Target Job from the Other Side of the Desk

This is where you deconstruct your collection of job postings to understand exactly how employers think about, prioritize, and describe the deliverables of your job.

1. Start a new Word document, and name it "Primary Job TJD."
2. Under a first subhead, entitled "Target Job Titles," cut and paste the variations on the job title you are pursuing from your collection of job postings.

   When this is done, you will be able to decide on a target job title for your resume. This will come first on your resume immediately beneath your contact information. It will help your resume get discovered in database searches and, acting as a title, it will give any reader an immediate focus.
3. Add a second subhead entitled: "Experience/Responsibilities/Skills/Deliverables/Etc."

   Review your collection of job postings and find one requirement that is common to all six; of these six, choose the most complete description of that requirement, paste it under this second subhead, and put the number (6) in front of it to signify that it is common to all six job postings. Underneath it list any different keywords used in the other five job postings to describe this same requirement.

   Repeat these steps for any other requirements that are common to all six of your collected job postings, placing the number (6) alongside each one.
4. Repeat this process for all requirements that are common to five of the six job postings, then four of the six postings, and so on down the line, finishing with those requirements that are unique to a single job posting.

At the end of this first part of the *TJD* sequence you will be able to read the document and say to yourself, "When employers are looking for _____, these are the job titles they use; this is the order in which they prioritize the importance of their needs, these are the skills and educational requirements they look for, and these are the words they use to describe them." As you read through your *TJD* document, the story your resume needs to tell will be laid out before you.

Step #4: Problem-Solving and Intelligent Enthusiasm

PROBLEM-SOLVING

At their most elemental level, all jobs are the same—they focus on *problem identification, prevention, and solution.* Once you have professional experience, your ability to identify and solve the problems that crop up in your target job will become a big part of turning job interviews into job offers. At the start of your career you don't have this experience to draw on, but there are a couple of things you can do.

> Most new grads have experience. Did you work part-time? Were you a member of a fraternity/sorority or other association? Did you actively participate in or chair a committee? Did you have an internship? Did you work on projects in the classroom? Were you an athlete or involved in activities that required planning/training/team involvement?
>
> **Jacqui Barrett-Poindexter, MRW, CEIP,** Partner and Chief Career Writer, *www.careertrend.net*

First of all, using your alumni and LinkedIn networks (for more on this see Chapters 4–6), identify either people doing this job now or managers of people doing this job. Approach them for connections and, after establishing contact, ask for this advice:

- What are the problems at the heart of this job, the ones that crop up every week? How should these problems be handled when they occur?
- How do these problems affect the success of the employee and department? How do they affect the profitability of the company?
- How do you prevent these problems from arising in the first place?

Ask these questions of half a dozen people and you will begin to get a profile of how a consummate professional in your field goes about her job. Even without experience tackling and preventing these problems, you can use the insights you gather to show an understanding of the job that other candidates simply will not have. You can and will use this knowledge in e-mails, in your resume, in networking conversations, and at interviews.

This understanding of the importance of *problem identification, prevention, and solution,* as it applies to your profession, is a powerful tool that will propel your career through the years. You can also use it to great effect in your first job search.

Intelligent Enthusiasm

In a tightly run job race, when there is nothing to choose between top candidates, the offer always goes to the candidate who demonstrates the most *intelligent enthusiasm* about the job. Your understanding of what is at the very core of your target job—in fact the very reasons your job exists—and your precocious knowledge of how these issues should be handled and how they can be prevented will become a demonstration of *intelligent enthusiasm* that hiring managers are going to respond to very positively.

If you really know the problems the job presents, understand how these problems impact the department and the company, and have some idea of how they can be prevented, you already have a very powerful argument for your candidacy, not to mention a leg up on your entry-level competition. You are now in a position not just to tell employers, but to *show* them, through your behavior and your communications, that you are enthusiastic about gaining practical experience dealing with professional problems, that you are engaged and willing to learn, and that you really understand why the job exists. All this will dramatically differentiate you from other entry-level candidates.

Step #5: Problems and Achievements

Writing your resume without work experience requires you to identify those activities that you did as a volunteer or as a student. When you look at the job vacancy announcement, think of those skills that can directly translate into the required duties and responsibilities listed in the employer's job description.

Sultan Camp, Military Transition and Social Network Specialist, *www.zeiders.com*

Even when you have no experience you can expect interviewers to ask about the challenges you have faced in life and how you dealt with them. You'll hear this referred to as a *behavioral* interview technique, meaning that discovering how you behaved in a given situation in the past is a reasonable predictor of how you are likely to behave in difficult situations in the future. For example you might be asked about situations when:

- Things didn't work out well (but did in the end)
- Things didn't work out well ever, and what you learned
- You had to make unpopular decisions
- You developed new ways of doing something
- You improved something that was already working well
- You fixed something broken

Think through the examples you might use in response to such queries. Then make a list of your life's achievements and the problems you had to overcome to achieve them. Work-, volunteer-, and community-related examples are best, but they can come from any aspect of your life. Come up with a couple of examples of projects that went wrong and couldn't be fixed, and what you learned from them that you can apply in the future. Stay away from legal and moral problems: They might not go where you want.

No work experience? I highly recommend that you become active in volunteer work that benefits the community with respected community-based organizations—ideally nonprofit organizations.

Valentino B. Martinez, President, *www.managementconsultants.us*

Give some thought to these examples now as you do *TJD,* and come back to them when you are preparing for job interviews. This may seem like a lot of work, but the *TJD* is not just important for this chapter—it is the foundation of everything you will learn in this book. No other chapter of this book demands nearly as much work as this one, but that's only because all the other chapters rely on the hard work you do here. *TJD* is the foundation not only for resumes and cover letters but for social networking, successful interviews, and the development of a *professional persona* that will carry you to career success.

Step #6: *Transferable Skills* and *Professional Values*

Almost everybody has that restaurant job during college, so make sure you punch up the job description to really articulate the transferable skills.

Caroline Dowd-Higgins, Career Director, Maurer School of Law; CBS Radio Host, *www.carolinedowdhiggins.com*

The final step of *TJD* is to review each of the skills/responsibilities/ deliverables of the job one last time to identify which of the *transferable skills* and *professional values* will help you execute your responsibilities in each of the target job's responsibilities. Unless you've worked as an intern, you probably don't have any experience with your target job, but there are ways around this. You can ask your networking contacts who hold or held the job you're aiming for. You can get information on the work from Google and niche job websites, and you can get involved with your professional community by joining relevant groups on LinkedIn, professional associations, and your alumni association (see Chapters 4–6 for more on this).

Once you complete and review your *TJD*, you will have a clear idea of the way employers think about, prioritize, and express their needs for this job, and this will help you write a resume that gets pulled from resume databases and resonates with recruiters and hiring managers. You'll know what they'll need to ask about at interviews and, beyond the hard *technical skills*, you will have a good idea of the person they want to hire. And when you apply what you learn from the *TJD* exercise to your first professional job, you will establish job security and open doors to the inner circles that exist in every department and company—and the inner circle is where job security (such as it is) and all those plum projects, raises, and promotions live. It will take time and it would be easy to cut corners or just skip it, but this is your career and this is your life: It is up to you now, make the choice that is right for your long-term success and happiness.

Building Your Resume

Once you have a clearly defined target job, you can look back into your work history, such as it is, and pull out the experiences that best reflect your ability to do this job. The tool to help you gather the right information is the Resume Questionnaire, which you can find and download from *www.knockemdead.com*: Look for the Downloads tab on the navigation bar.

> Draw upon anything and everything you have done in the past. This can include summer and school-year internships, volunteer work and mission trips, extracurricular activities, sports and clubs, entrepreneurial ventures, social media and blogging, consulting, speaking.
>
> **Chris Perry**, Brand and Marketing Generator, *www.careerrocketeer.com*

Five Rules for Building Great Resumes

1. YOUR E-MAIL ADDRESS AS A MARKETING TOOL

Now might be a good time to retire those college-era addresses like: *binkypoo@yahoo.com, bigboy@hotmail.com,* and *DDdoll@live.com.* Never in the history of job search have more opportunities been wasted by so many thanks to something so silly.

A profession-focused e-mail address acts as a headline that tells the recipient who is calling and offers some idea of what the communication is about. You should create an e-mail address that speaks to your professional identity, for example: *SystemAnalyst@hotmail.com* or *Accountant@yahoo.com.* These will be taken, but don't just start typing random numbers. Try adding relevant information like your town, zip code, or area code: *SystemAnalyst_11579@hotmail.com.* In a competitive job search, the little things can make a big difference, and the *way* you introduce yourself is one of them.

2. SETTLE ON A TARGET JOB TITLE

Always use a target job title. The target job title appears at the top of your resume, immediately after your contact information. It's a headline for the whole document. This will help your resume's database performance and give readers an immediate focus on who you are and what you do. The logical title will emerge from your *TJD* work.

3. INCLUDE A PERFORMANCE PROFILE

Follow your target job title with a brief summary of what you have to offer; this should carry its own heading.

If you have any relevant work experience, use "Performance Profile" as your heading. Take the top four or five requirements for the job (as determined by your *TJD* exercise) and write three to six lines that speak to your ability to execute the most important requirements of the job. Wherever possible, use the words and phrases you captured in the *TJD.* By using these specific words, you simultaneously demonstrate your grasp of what's important in this job and sing the song the spiders want to hear (see earlier in this chapter for more on search engine spiders and their mysterious ways).

If you don't have much relevant work experience, use the headline "Summary." Take the same top four or five requirements for the job, as determined by your *TJD* exercise, and write three to six lines that speak to either your ability to do the work or to your desire for the opportunity to do it. Wherever possible use the words and phrases you captured in the *TJD*. Since you can't talk about how you've done the work, you can at least talk in a way that demonstrates your thorough understanding of what the work involves. And there's an added bonus: The spiders can't tell whether you've *done* _____ or are just saying that you would *like to do* _____! As long as you use the keywords, they let you in the door.

4. Make the Best Possible Use of Resume Real Estate

A Core Competencies/Professional Skills section follows the Performance Summary/Profile. You identified a wide selection of the competencies required for this job in your *TJD*, and this part of your resume should list as many of them as you possess. You might also include any other skills that you know to be relevant based on your social networking outreach to professionals doing the job you want to do. As a recent graduate, you identify professional skills you have developed in school and in part-time, volunteer, entrepreneurial, and community jobs. You can also include computer skills, Internet communication tools, and social media platforms with which you are familiar. *Transferable skills* and *professional values* are commonly used in both job postings and in recruiters' database searches, so if you feel the claims would be valid, you should include these skills.

This helps database visibility because it guarantees you are using the words employers use. By getting them near the top of the page you ensure that they carry more weight with the algorithms of database search engines.

Following a target job title and Performance Profile or Summary, your Core Competency/Professional Skills section lists all the skills required to execute the responsibilities of the job. For the reader evaluating your resume, each word or phrase acts as a headline for a topic to be addressed at the interview and increases the odds of that interview happening, so make sure to customize this section to the particulars of each job description.

A Core Competency/Professional Skills section positions all the critical information a recruiter would need in the first half of the first page. This concern for user-friendliness succinctly demonstrates your *critical thinking* and *written communication* skills.

Here is an example from a recent graduate. Despite not having any professional work experience, you get a very strong idea that here is a serious contender.

Analyst Environmental Science/Geographic Information Systems (GIS)

Summary

Talented, analytical geography graduate with a **strong academic background** in Geographic Information Systems and **multiple certifications covering a full range of skills related to GIS, environmental safety, and rescue measures.** Organized professional with exceptional follow-through abilities and attention to detail. Advanced problem-solving skills with the capacity to multitask in fast-paced environments. **Self-motivated and disciplined with a desire to succeed, as evidenced by successfully working full-time throughout full-time undergraduate studies.** Experience coordinating with clients, city planning departments, and subcontractors during planning and building phases of projects.

✓ Ability to record accurate **field notes** using **multiple software** programs.

✓ Solid foundation in **cost assessment** analysis.

✓ Develops and implements improved procedures to **resolve efficiency issues.**

✓ Advanced analytical and **problem-solving skills.**

✓ **Proven background in leading teams** in detail-oriented environments.

Professional Skills

- Project management
- Research analysis and reporting
- P & L management
- Disaster preparation and recovery
- Word, Excel, PowerPoint
- Windows XP, Mac OS
- Arc GIS, Arc INFO, Arc Catalog
- GIS Map interpretation and analysis
- Environmental resource management
- Team-building and leadership skills
- Land use planning
- Excellent time-management skills
- Plans and develops business proposals
- Business development

You can, and wherever relevant you *should*, repeat keywords throughout the body of your resume within the context of each job in which you used them, at least doubling the number of relevant keywords and further improving your resume's performance with the resume database search engines.

5. HIGHLIGHT YOUR PROFESSIONAL EXPERIENCE

Paid jobs, internships, and volunteer work can all qualify as relevant work experience for an entry-level professional. You should include company names and employment dates.

How to Build a Database-Visible and Visually Accessible Resume

Once you have established the resume's focus with a *TJD* and gathered all the relevant information within the resume questionnaire, it's time to start assembling everything into a document that takes on the appearance of a resume. A productive resume has certain component parts and a fairly standard layout that help it achieve the triple goals of:

- Visibility in database searches
- Rapid visual accessibility to the quick initial visual reviews conducted by recruiters
- Rapid visual accessibility of the job-relevant detail required to satisfy a hiring manager

On the following page you will find a resume layout template with optimal visual accessibility. You would do well to emulate it.

After you write your resume, you still need to edit it. Make sure to use legible 11- or 12-point fonts. You also need to make sure that your resume focuses on what the manager wants, not what *you* want. We cover what *you* want in Chapter 11.

Resume Length

Your resume should be succinct and focused on a specific target job. You should strive to keep to the point and try to keep it to one page, but if you need to go to a second page, that's fine. You have probably been told that your resume must not exceed one page, but this is long outdated advice.

Your resume has two jobs to do. Firstly, it needs to be data-dense enough with keywords so that corporate recruiters can actually find it and pull it for review from amongst the millions of other resumes that fill commercial resume databases. Secondly, it has to speak clearly about your fit for a specific job.

Resume Layout template. This is one way to lay out all your resume information. Choose your final template from the Knock 'em Dead resume templates at *www.knockemdead.com*.

Name

| Address | Telephone | E-mail address |

Pharmaceutical Sales

A target job title, like the above example, helps database visibility and gives focus to the reader.

Performance Profile

A maximum of five lines of text, which can be followed by a second paragraph or list of bullets. Take the most common requirements from your TJD and rewrite them as Performance Profile. This helps database visibility and creates immediate resonance with reader's eyes.

Professional Skills/Core Competencies

A list of all the skills you identified in the TJD. Repeat each skill listed here in context of the jobs where it was applied. This increases database visibility and gives the reader immediate focus, "Oh he can talk about all of these things . . ." Example:

4-Handed Dentistry	Infection Control	Preventative Care
Oral Surgery/Extraction	Casts/Impressions	Emergency Treatment
Root Canals	Diagnostic X-Rays	Instrument Sterilization
Prosthetics/Restorations	Teeth Whitening	Radiology

Technical Competencies

An optional category depending on your technical capabilities and professional relevance.

Professional Experience

Employer's name   Dates
The company's focus
Job Title

If you are going to bold/caps anything, draw attention to what is most important: your job title.

Employer's name   Dates
The company's focus
Job Title

Employer's name   Dates
The company's focus
Job Title

Contact information at top of each page. Keep your resume tightly edited but do not worry about page count. Reason: Jobs are more complex than they used to be, the additional info increases database performance and reader won't mind if resume is telling a relevant story.

Employer's name   Dates
The companies focus
Job title
Repeat employment history as necessary.

Education
Educational credentials usually come at the resume's end, but may come at front if this is a critical professional requirement (Medicine, Law) or is your strongest credential.

Licenses/Professional Accreditations
May come at front if these credentials are critical credentials, especially relevant, or highlight an important strength.

Ongoing Professional Education

Professional Organizations/Affiliations

Publications, Patents, Speaking

Languages
Add them to the end of the Performance Profile and repeat them here.

Military service

Extra curricular interests
If they relate to the job. Sports demonstrate fitness; chess etc. denotes analytical skills; and community involvement are all relevant.

(References)
Never list references on your resume. Employers *assume* that your references are available, but it certainly doesn't hurt to end with a bold statement:

References Available on Request
Or
Excellent references available on request
Or
My references will verify everything in this resume

On top of this, technology has both increased the complexity of all jobs and created a whole new set of skills we all must have to survive in the professional world of today. Together, all these issues mean that you have more to say than the recently graduated candidate of ten or fifteen years ago, and if you don't say it for fear of your resume exceeding one page, then it may never see the light of day.

On the other hand, if you write a data-dense resume packed with the keywords recruiters will use to find it, it will get pulled from the resume databases for review. When this happens, do you think that when the recruiter realizes that your resume goes beyond one page, she will say, "Wow, this candidate really looks like he can do the job, but we couldn't possibly interview him, because he exceeds the one page resume rule that was established in 1973"? Of course not.

If the first page of your resume is tightly focused and contains a Target Job Title, a Performance Summary or Performance Profile built on the priorities you identified with *TJD*, and a Professional Skills/Core Competency section packed with relevant keywords, you will have the reader's attention by the time she gets halfway down the first page. When the first page makes a convincing argument, a second page will be read carefully because the evidence of the first suggests that it will be relevant.

Bear this in mind as your career progresses: The need for more detailed resumes means that your first job *change* will almost certainly require a two-page resume, and by the time you have ten years' experience, you will almost certainly be running to three pages.

Controlling Resume Length

While length doesn't matter as much as it used to, you should still make every effort to maintain focus and an "if in doubt, cut it out" editing approach. If you're having trouble keeping your resume pruned to a manageable length, remember that you can add the information you must cut to a more detailed social networking profile at LinkedIn.com or Facebook.com (social networking is addressed in Chapters 4–6).

The word *resume* is French for "summary," not life story. Don't state the obvious. If you worked as a cashier, you don't need to say "operated a cash register."

Rich Grant, Director of Career Services, *www.thomas.edu*

Social Networking Links

Recruiters like to see social networking links on your resume to find out more about you. So if there is "nice to have" but not "must have" information on your resume that is pushing you onto another page, cut it and add it to your LinkedIn profile. Only add a social media link to your profile if that link is entirely professional in content and reflects the same person as your resume.

On the next page you will find a good example of a *Knock 'em Dead* resume: job-targeted, coordinated Performance Profile and Core Competency sections with keywords repeated in context, a clean businesslike layout, and appropriate font choice. Resume templates and custom-built resumes like this are available at *www.knockemdead.com*.

The Video Resume

A video resume is not meant to replace a traditional resume or social media profile, but to add another weapon to your arsenal. It is best used to demonstrate what you can't show on paper; everyone can write about his superior *communication skills*, amazing personality, and unparalleled professional drive, but a video gives you the opportunity to prove it.

A video resume is a great way to set yourself apart. On video, you can show off the intangibles that don't show on your traditional resume like personality, passion, and communication skills.

Josh Tolan, CEO, *www.sparkhire.com*

Patricia Smith

125 Main Street #555, Corona, California 92880
(505) 555-1212   Smith13@aol.com

Analyst Environmental Science/Geographic Information Systems (GIS)

Performance Profile

Talented, analytical geography graduate with a **strong academic background** in Geographic Information Systems and **multiple certifications covering a full range of skills related to GIS, environmental safety, and rescue measures**. Organized professional with exceptional follow-through abilities and attention to detail. Advanced problem-solving skills with the capability to accurately multitask in fast-paced environments. **Self-motivated, disciplined with a desire to succeed as evidenced by attending college full-time while working full-time.** Experience coordinating with clients, city planning departments, and subcontractors during planning and building phases of projects.

- ✓ Ability to record accurate **field notes** using **multiple software** programs.
- ✓ Solid foundation in **cost assessment** analysis.
- ✓ Develop and implement improved procedures to **resolve efficiency issues**.
- ✓

Professional Skills

• Project management	• GIS Map interpretation and analysis
• Research analysis and reporting	• Environmental resource management
• P & L management	• Teambuilding and leadership skills
• Disaster preparation and recovery	• Land use planning
• Word, Excel, PowerPoint	• Excellent time management skills

Professional Experience

J.M. Ventures: The Catch Restaurant; Taps Fish House & Brewery, Anaheim, California
07–Present
   Fine Dining Server recruited to implement the company's new wine club resulting in a successful increase in wine sales. Wine club was awarded Best of Award Program by *Wine Spectator* magazine.

- Increased knowledge of macroclimates of regional wines and sensitivity of climatic characteristics which affect the specific grape varietal grown and subsequent vintage.
- Anticipated guest needs while utilizing excellent communication and time management skills.
- **Employee of the month, March 2010.**

Falcon Tile & Stone, Inc., Placentia, California
05–07
   Project Manager for company specializing in natural stone slab fabrications and installations.

- Developed prices and business proposals for homeowners and business owners.
- Increased business development through negotiating and closing proposals.
- Assisted P&L management by budgeting materials purchased and managing labor for installations.

Education & Training

Bachelor of Arts, Geography, California State University, Long Beach, California
2010
Areas of emphasis: GIS, natural resource management

Intermediate GIS, GIS cartography and base map development, GIS in environment technology.

Video resumes have been around for over thirty years and have never before played a meaningful role in job search, but with new technology I think we are entering an era when the video resume—alongside your traditional resume and LinkedIn profile—may come into its own as the third primary marketing tool.

The Story You Tell and How It Should Be Told

A video resume gives you an opportunity to look a recruiter in the eyes and tell him why you are the one. It's a chance to tell the recruiter why you want and deserve that job more than other contenders. Given the basic skills, recruiters want to see passion and personality and that *intelligent enthusiasm* we talk about throughout the book. The candidate who shows this drive immediately differentiates herself. Don't just repeat your resume on video: Show and tell me why you're different and better for the job. If I have resumes with similar qualifications, which will be the case, seeing and hearing you in a well-structured video resume could well be the tiebreaker.

You created a summary for your resume based on your *TJD*, and later in the book you will learn how to answer one of the first questions you will face at an interview, "Tell me about yourself." You can use this information to create an "elevator pitch" on why you should be hired. An elevator pitch is your most concise breakdown of your value proposition; its name comes from the thought that this is what you would say if you found yourself in an elevator with your target customer and only had those few moments to convince him. Your video resume will make the same points as your resume, but I will see your professional dress and demeanor, hear your *verbal communication skills* in action, and hopefully feel your *intelligent enthusiasm*.

Less is more: This is not a movie production. A sixty-second self-directed video is all you need. As a recruiter, I want to see, in a direct, professional manner, why I should hire you. Look me in the eye (or in this case the camera lens and imagine it's me) and tell me why you should be hired as if I were in the room with you.

You can try this yourself, hire a video editor, or record a video resume on a webcam/IOS/Android mobile device and use the tools of a website like SparkHire.com (probably the premier company in this area) to make it shine.

RESOURCES There is much more to be done in crafting an effective resume; this is just a start. Here are some further resources to help you with the step-by-step creation of your resume:

- You can find a downloadable MS Word resume questionnaire at *www.knockemdead.com* that will help you gather all the necessary information to build a killer resume.
- For a full discussion of all aspects of resume building, see *Knock 'em Dead Resumes*, latest edition, both online and in your local bookstore.
- Additionally, see *Knock 'em Dead Resumes & Templates*, which comes with everything you find in *Knock 'em Dead Resumes*, plus 110 ready-to-use MS Word resume templates. This enhanced version is available only at *www.knockemdead.com*.
- You can also invest in a professionally written resume at *www.knockemdead.com*.

PART II
NETWORKING

CHAPTER 4

How to Build Networks for Today and Tomorrow

Networking is a powerful job search and career-management tool. In this and the following two chapters, you will learn how to harness networking to your every job-search strategy, and as a result, your career will launch successfully and you'll be able to exert more control over your professional destiny moving forward.

> An effective job search requires a multifaceted approach. You cannot sit at home on your computer firing off resumes and hope your phone rings.
>
> **Rich Grant,** Director of Career Services, *www.thomas.edu*

The Hiring Process

Companies assess their staffing needs up to twelve months in advance, so the interviews you go on this year were mostly planned and budgeted toward the end of last year. Hiring budgets usually open at the start of the new calendar year with hires staggered throughout the year. The early part of every year usually has plenty of opportunity, and entry-level hires are often staggered to coincide with graduation and the following months.

> In May and December, inboxes are flooded with new grad resumes. If yours is less clear or concise than your competition, you are putting yourself at a disadvantage.
>
> **Sean Koppelman**, President, *www.thetalentmagnet.com*

Recruitment starts with, "Who do we know?", and this is where internships and involvement with campus societies can be a big help. Internships give you real work experience, references, and exposure to working professionals for your network. Likewise, being active in campus societies makes you visible to campus recruiters, who claim they make their best entry-level professional hires from these societies way before the arrival of career days on campus. Only when this fails do companies start to post jobs on job banks and social networking sites.

> An employer will likely post a job opening utilizing free resources first. There are numerous free job boards. A good list of them can be found on the home page of ZipRecruiter.com.
>
> **Tegan Acree**, Founder, *www.hiringforhope.org*

Intelligent Networking

In this new world of work, you'll need to use a number of different job search approaches and learn to integrate networking strategy into each of them. A lot—but not all—of networking has moved online, so successful professional networking means having active accounts on social networking sites like LinkedIn.com and Facebook.com. Your online presence will help you develop networks that alert you to jobs and perhaps provide introductions to those jobs while also making you visible to recruiters.

For networking to be productive, you need to form relationships with people in your prospective profession and industry at many levels. Almost anyone in your profession, industry, or target location can be useful regardless of title or experience. However, the contacts who will be most helpful—*the high-value target job titles*—will fall into the following categories:

1. Those who are one to three title levels above you; these are the people most likely to hire you both now and in the future.
2. Those who hold a similar job title, but have more experience (that's just about everyone).
3. Those who work in the same profession or industry but in other areas of expertise. People in this third group are slightly less valuable because their jobs mean they are not as closely connected to the people and titles involved in the recruitment and selection cycle for someone with your target job title, but they still have reasonable potential of being able to give you leads and referrals.

Networking depends on goodwill, so with all your networking contacts try to build a relationship by finding common ground. You can initiate relationships by asking for advice, and many people will give you a few minutes of their time. However, you will develop the best relationships by reaching out to others with help and advice, because when you offer good things, forging a relationship with you becomes important to the other person.

How can you help and advise when you don't know anyone and have no professional expertise? The answer is surprisingly painless. Throughout your job search, you are going to come across a boatload of job openings for people with more experience than you. Instead of just passing these by and moving on to the next one, *you share these job leads, which are inappropriate for your own use, with people for whom they might be appropriate.* We will talk more about this as we build your network.

Having a "connection" doesn't mean you know that person or that they are obligated to help you. It's up to you to build a mutually beneficial and reciprocal relationship.

Lori Ruff, CEO, *www.integratedalliances.com*

Professional Networking Etiquette

Up till now, you have been given all sorts of advice by parents, teachers, and professors, and that advice has kept on coming regardless of how you behaved on receiving it. Your experience in the professional world will be very different.

Professional networking is about sharing and giving, a *process* of building relationships over time, and the effectiveness of the networks you build will reflect the effort you put into their development. Advice, assistance, introductions, referrals, and camaraderie—these things are not free in the professional world; they depend on give-and-take, and on a degree of courtesy with which you might not be familiar. Watch how professionals interact with each other, both online and in-person, then model yourself on the best examples. Use people's names and remember "please" and "thank you" or the professional networks that are so important to this job search and your long-term success will fail to materialize.

> Your bio and daily activity say a lot about your professionalism and judgment.
>
> **Tim Tyrell-Smith,** Founder, *www.timsstrategy.com*

You are not new to meeting people through your social networks, but you are probably new to networking with professional intent. Your goal is to meet and build relationships with people who can have a positive impact on your career, because of who they are and what they do. At first this can be intimidating, because it requires you to go outside your comfort zone, asking complete strangers for help and offering help in return.

Fortunately, you have a couple of factors in your favor. First, everyone remembers what it was like trying to get his first job, and so everyone is predisposed to help you. And second, everyone likes to give advice and be seen as an authority figure. You can and must use this knowledge to your advantage. *Make people feel good about helping you and you'll find yourself getting more help.*

> People aren't looking to help you. But people are willing to help you if you make it easy for them.
>
> **Carl Nielson,** Principal, *www.careercoachingforstudents.net*

Two Types of Networks

There are two major types of networks: professional and community. You will build your professional network with people already working in your prospective field from online social networking sites, college and high school alumni associations, and membership in professional associations. As time goes by, you'll add managers, coworkers, and professional colleagues.

Community networks are built on family and relatives; friends and social interest groups; civic and spiritual associations; and service industry acquaintances such as your banker, lawyer, plumber, etc. These groups will grow over the years through evolving family relationships, the roots you put down as an adult in the community where you live, and the people you meet through your changing hobbies and personal interests.

Social Networking

> Employers and recruiters do look at all your social media pages. Be conscious of what you post and what others post about you.
>
> **Caroline Dowd-Higgins,** Career Director, Maurer School of Law; CBS Radio Host, *www.carolinedowdhiggins.com*

Social networking via sites like Facebook and LinkedIn has transformed the way many people communicate. While Facebook is arguably the most visited website in the world, it is largely aimed at interactions between friends. LinkedIn, on the other hand, is the most important professional networking site for making connections and becoming visible, both within your professional community and to corporate recruiters, headhunters, and hiring managers.

If you're not a member of LinkedIn, go register while you watch the boob tube tonight. Create a basic profile and make your first connection: Put my name in the search box, say you know me through *Knock 'em Dead*, and invite me to connect.

Your Social Media Profile

A couple of suggestions of Twitter lists to follow:

#internpro – **Monday at 9 P.M. EST**

#jobhuntchat – **Monday at 10 P.M. EST**

#genychat – **Wednesday at 9 P.M. EST**

Phyllis Mufson, Career Coach, *www.phyllismufson.com*

Although LinkedIn is known as a "social networking" site, no one has any illusions that it is anything but the world's premier place for professional networking. Remember at all times that you are becoming involved for professional reasons; this should inform everything you say about yourself on your profile, because LinkedIn is the place where you begin to forge a professional identity, and a place where you are likely to be active for many years to come.

You start building your LinkedIn profile by simply cutting and pasting your resume into the different sections. Resumes are typically written in the third person, so you'll need to rewrite it for your LinkedIn profile using the first person, because social media profiles need to sound as if you are talking directly to the reader.

Your profile should tell the same story as your resume and then, if there is more to say, expand on it, giving more detail about your professional self. Look to see if you have any information from your *TJD* or from the resume questionnaire (*www.my.knockemdead.com/*

downloads) that you didn't use in your resume. You can also add additional details about any school, volunteer, intern, community, or church projects that speak to your professional skills and credentials for your target job. Looking back to the resume writing process, you may remember having to cut information in order to streamline your resume. Some of the deathless prose that ended up on the cutting-room floor can be used here if it is relevant and adds to the story you wish to tell.

> All eyes go to the profile image first. Does your profile pic show you to be likable? Confident? Professional? If not, invest the money to get some headshots and candids done . . . it's well worth the effort!
>
> **Mark Babbitt,** CEO and Founder, *www.youtern.com*

Resume Versus Social Media Profile

The technology advances that gave birth to the Internet and the social media phenomenon have changed the way companies recruit and people find jobs. Social media sites have given recruiters another great source for finding candidates, and job seekers another great way to make themselves visible, but this does not herald the death of the resume. As my esteemed friend and colleague Joyce Lain Kennedy says:

> The online profile is not a customized document, but is more like a one-size-fits-all pitch posted on a digital billboard that's located on a busy information superhighway and seen, hopefully, by hordes of unknown viewers.
>
> **Joyce Lain Kennedy,** Syndicated Columnist and Author, *www.sunfeatures.com*

A good social media profile on a social networking site makes you visible to corporate recruiters; for these recruiters, social media sites are just new kinds of resume databases that they can search with keywords. A properly executed social media profile makes you more visible, but it is passive, because people have to look for it. It is an important job-search tool, but it does not guarantee that you will be seen, or be seen by the right people.

Your resume, on the other hand, is both an active and a passive job search tool.

1. **A passive job search tool:** Upload your resume into resume databases and it operates like a social media profile, making you visible to people who are actively looking for professionals like you in that particular database.

2. **An active job search tool:** You can customize your resume to one specific job or even to each company you approach. You can have different resumes for different jobs you wish to pursue, and you can send such carefully customized resumes directly to the recruiters and hiring managers you most want to talk to.

You live in a world where there are very few either/or choices anymore, and the resume versus social media issue certainly isn't one of them. One won't replace the other, because your resume and social media profile(s) do different jobs for you. You can't do without either; with this first job search, having both will help you land your first position, and going forward, your LinkedIn profile can become a vital tool for enhancing your credibility and visibility.

Keywords

One of the ways you will start to make professional contacts is through database searches. For example, if you were looking for other accountants on LinkedIn, you might try the obvious: "accountant." Looking at the individual profiles in the results of your search, you should notice the frequency and positioning of the keyword you are using—in this case "accountant"—in the listing. For instance, in searching for accountants, LinkedIn values "accountant" more in titles to sections of your profile than it does in the body copy of that section. Just as you will search for others on LinkedIn using keywords, other professionals, corporate recruiters, hiring managers, and sometimes headhunters will be using keywords to search for you. These keyword searches are weighted, which means that the LinkedIn search engine values certain words appearing in some places more than it values the same word in other places.

> Because 92 percent of employers use Twitter, Facebook, and LinkedIn, you should create profiles and be visible on all three social media sites.
>
> **Sandra Ingemansen, CPRW,** Principal, *www.resume-strategies.com*

LinkedIn has lots of great advice on making your profile visible. Follow this advice, then do "people" searches (the "people" search box is prominent on your home page) using the keywords that identify your target job. When you look at the individual results of your search, notice how LinkedIn helpfully highlights the keyword(s) that you need to use frequently and also shows you where to place them for maximum search-engine visibility.

Your Profile as a Long-Term Marketing Tool

Over the years, your profile will become your face to the professional world. So if you want to manage your professional destiny and think of your career in the terms of MeInc, your LinkedIn profile should be treated as a MeInc marketing tool: Its job is to consistently promote the visibility and credibility of the ever-evolving brand that is your *professional persona*. Consequently, your profile on LinkedIn will continue to change and grow over the years to reflect your professional growth and evolving brand. If you also use other professional networking sites, your profiles on them should be compatible with your LinkedIn profile. All your profiles don't need to be the same, but they shouldn't be contradictory in any way.

We find that over 50 percent of LinkedIn profiles have more jobs and/or different dates than the corresponding resume. This is a job-offer killer.

Roger Lear, President, *www.orlandojobs.com*

LinkedIn Groups

In addition to job postings, LinkedIn has links to job boards, local social events, and thousands of special interest groups, many for job hunters and many more that are profession-specific. Belonging to groups and connecting with other members is one of the easiest and most efficient ways to build a job-search network.

Comment on something specific that another person is saying. Be polite and detailed; add value. Don't over-interact. Step lightly into the conversational water at first.

Jacqui Barrett-Poindexter, MRW, CEIP, Partner and Chief Career Writer, *www.careertrend.net*

To start building a job search–relevant professional network, join LinkedIn groups that are relevant to your target job and profession. Become a visible part of that group by joining in the conversation and approaching other group members to add to your network. You do this by:

- *Reading the group discussion posts and adding comments.* You probably can't add substance, but you can make comments like this: "I just received my accounting degree from _____ and am entering the professional world, and this was really helpful." Notice that along with the gradual visibility that comes from making posts, flattering the original poster, and getting noticed by all the other people who comment, you have also announced your credentials and stated who you are and what you are looking for without being crass and asking for help finding work.

Get others to talk about themselves. Ask for their opinions, insights, and professional perspectives. Listening is a skill-set that few master professionally, whether a recent grad or a seasoned executive. It's a rare trait.

Kevin Kermes, Founder, *www.careerattraction.com*

It's a no-brainer to subsequently approach each of these discussion posters to connect with you, using your common membership in the group as a bond.

- *Post discussions of your own.* As mentioned elsewhere, you can get the most mileage by posting blogs and articles from influential sources, which others will comment on. You should read the professional press and blogs, and when you see something that seems to have real relevance to your profession, post a link to the article. Then make link requests to anyone who comments.

- *Post questions of your own.* Not questions about finding a job or employers, but issues about the challenges of the job. There's an easy way to make sure the questions you ask come off as professional and not self-serving. Remember the discussion of *critical thinking* in Chapter 2? You learned that at the most basic level all jobs are about *anticipating, preventing, and solving problems.* When you sound like a professional colleague interested in improving skills and understanding, or finding *solutions* to common *problems*, your questions will have the right tone.

Done right, LinkedIn groups can be a great way to become known in an industry or interest area. You can build expertise as well as social credibility with new people simply by making valuable comments or sharing your opinion on a subject.

Tim Tyrell-Smith, Founder, *www.timsstrategy.com*

How to Make the Most Useful Connections

Anyone in a profession-specific group is potentially a good contact, but your highest potential–reward connections are people:

- With a similar title to the one you are pursuing, but with more experience.
- With management titles one to three levels above the position you are seeking.

Look for people who fit these criteria in the membership rosters of the groups you belong to, and approach them as connections using your shared group as an introduction and reason for your connection request.

You can also search the LinkedIn database by title, company, and other identifying factors to find useful professional connections for your network.

> When you ask someone to join your network, customize the default message. Explain why you want to connect with them.
>
> **Hannah Morgan,** Job Search Strategist, *www.careersherpa.net*

You can do the same thing with job titles and location, for example "accountant Illinois." With database searches, look for people who work in your target location and hold job titles relevant to your search. You won't know these people, but you can very often establish connectivity by identifying the groups they belong to; if they belong to groups you don't, just join the new group (LinkedIn allows membership in up to fifty groups).

There are many social networks geared to specific professions and special-interest groups, and the more these sites proliferate, the more specialized they become. As a serious professional you will have a presence on LinkedIn, and you probably already have a Facebook profile. Beyond this, go to Wikipedia and key in "social networks" for a complete listing. You'll find networking sites by special interest, country, language, sex, national origin, and more.

There is much to be said about social networks, but we can't cover it all in the space allowable. You'll find more resources at the end of the chapter and on the blog at *www.knockemdead.com.*

Alumni Associations

Because you're a recent graduate, alumni association membership can be immensely helpful to you. Your college alumni association can put you within reach of thousands of other graduates working in your target profession, holding positions on the highest rungs of the professional ladder and in the very companies you would consider as employers.

Because of the shared college experience, these are people who will invariably help you if they can, just as you would help them.

Your alumni association will have a membership database, and there will almost certainly be a job-search network and quite possibly job postings. You will want to focus on alumni with your degree, working in your geographic target area, and/or who work or have worked with companies that you wish to target.

> Use alumni networks and seek out people in the industry you wish to pursue who can share insight/information that can give you an edge. These are the same people who can also provide introductions that may lead to job offers.
>
> **Sean Koppelman**, President, *www.thetalentmagnet.com*

When approaching alumni—or for that matter any networking contact—it is always best to have a clear agenda in mind. This should not be, "You don't know me from a hole in the ground, but can you help me get a job?", but more along the lines of, "We both graduated from _____. I graduated this year, and seeing your experience I wondered if I could ask your advice about [*an accounting matter*]?" Make the request simple and easily answered. Your exchanges might be by e-mail, by phone, in person, or a combination of the three. Once your query is satisfied and you have said thank you in a thoughtful manner, ask if you can send your resume; this gets your resume into the hands of someone working in the same general professional area, and you can subsequently follow up with questions about leads. Intersperse any requests for assistance with other contacts containing interesting professional information or job postings that might be of interest to your contact. Doing things in this order creates an atmosphere of give and take and increases the odds of your contact wanting to help you.

Alumni association membership will empower you to reach out to people with the same degree from the same school, working in companies all over the country and from the bottom to the top of the professional ladder. The site *www.alumni.net* will lead you to company, university, high school, and other alumni associations all over the world.

If alumni association membership is beyond your means, you can use LinkedIn as a fallback. For example, if you were an accountant who graduated from Georgia Southern, you could use "B.S. accounting Georgia Southern" as a search term. I just did it and got 340 results in my network alone.

Professional Networks

Professional association membership is one of the best tools for job search and long-term career management. All professions and/or industries have at least one and often many professional associations. You will want to identify associations that have members with your title (but with more experience) and members who hold job titles one, two, and three levels above your own, because these are the people who can give you the best advice and will have the most influence over your career today and for years to come. Remember: The person three titles above you today will be above you for all the decades to come until you reach the peak of your profession.

When you connect with your future professional community, you get to know all the most dedicated and best-connected professionals in your new field, and in turn you begin to become known by them. By belonging to a professional association, you'll also reinforce your image as someone who's serious about *professional commitment*. When you join a professional association, you should add membership to the end of your resume and to your LinkedIn and other social media profiles; doing so sends the right message about your professional identity and helps make you visible to like-minded people.

Stealth follow-up. If you know there is an industry-related function in your area that will likely be attended by some of the people you met, you might want to attend. They will appreciate someone who invests time in professional affairs.

Dr. Larry Chiagouris, Mentor, *www.thesecrettogettingajobaftercollege.com*

Among the many benefits of membership is the fact that association websites include job postings, because employers rightly believe that professional association members are all people who take their work very seriously and therefore are likely to make productive employees. You can and should respond directly to job postings you see by uploading your resume in the manner indicated, but because you are an association member, you can approach that job opening in other ways too. This can be a real boon. You have access to the association membership database and might well find another member—someone who works or worked for that company—who can give you inside information about the job, and perhaps even an introduction to a hiring authority within the company.

Association Meetings

The local chapter of the association you join will usually have monthly meetings. These are a great opportunity to form relationships with the most committed and best-connected people in your local professional landscape.

Don't worry about not having much to contribute at first. Meetings regularly feature training and professional accreditation programs that make you a more knowledgeable and therefore a more desirable employee; if you enroll in any form of professional accreditation training you can add it to your resume and social media profiles with an anticipated "graduation" date.

I can remember the first local association meeting I attended. I was living on Long Island, and I wanted to meet and get to know my local professional colleagues. I was also absolutely terrified. Fortunately I received some timeless good advice that will almost guarantee you acceptance and popularity:

New generations of professionals always get accused of lacking *humility*, a good *work ethic, pride* in their profession, and an *eagerness to learn*; you can use this to your advantage. Now think about this: You are nervous about going to association meetings because, unlike many of your peers, you have *humility*; but you are going anyway because, again unlike many of your peers, you have a good *work ethic, pride* in your profession, and an *eagerness to learn*.

You need a job more than anything in the world right now, but you don't want to be seen as opportunistic. While you have no professional knowledge to contribute, it's useful to know that associations function on volunteer power. This gives you the opportunity to make yourself visible by doing the work that needs to be done but that no one is eager to do. Before the meeting, help put out chairs and hand out paperwork and nametags; after the meeting, help move chairs, pick up the trash, and collect unused pads and papers.

You will be seen by and get to know the people in leadership positions, who will recognize your dedication and enthusiasm and give you encouragement. To these people—the people who count—you'll be seen as someone worth taking an interest in, and you'll get to know and learn from more senior people in your profession. You will be seen as a confident young professional who joined the association to understand your profession. You are polite, punctual, enthusiastic, and humble. You want to be seen as an up-and-comer who really cares about learning the business. Follow this advice and relationships will develop—and then job leads will follow.

Because associations function on volunteer power, once a few people in leadership positions know your name, you should also volunteer for one or more of the countless volunteer committees that help the organization run; this will help you get to know everyone. Of course, almost everything that is happening locally is also happening in the association's online groups, and you should establish a presence with these groups just as you do on LinkedIn.

Associations all have newsletters and blogs, and the website usually has job postings along with other useful intelligence about your professional community. The professional intelligence you gather on an association website can (with permission) be disseminated to your LinkedIn groups: "I'm a recent accounting graduate from _____ and saw this on the National Association of Accountants website last week. Thought it could be interesting . . ." You position yourself as someone more focused than your peers and demonstrate *teamwork* and *leadership* abilities, all in the same action.

For information about associations for your profession, the *Encyclopedia of Associations* is available online and at your local library. Or simply Google the name of your prospective profession or industry, followed by "association."

There are associations that cater to all kinds of special interest groups, for example women, many ethnicities, the multilingual, and the disabled. If you belong to any definable minority there is quite likely a vibrant professional group that connects you to others like you in your prospective profession. If you can find a niche association that's a fit, join that as well: It represents another, even more finely tuned network that you can nurture, and you may be sure that recruiters are checking out these special-interest professional associations regularly.

References

If you have any work experience at all, paid or volunteer, you should try to get references. If you've had internships in a relevant field, all the better. But even if you can only get an endorsement from your burger-flipping job, you should. When employers are filling a position for a recent graduate, comments about reliability, honesty, team spirit, flexibility, and your work ethic at McDonald's can serve you well. With no work experience to evaluate, it is challenging for recruiters and hiring managers to differentiate between entry-level candidates. This means that any time you can point to a use of the *transferable skills* and *professional values* in your educational, internship, or part-time work experience you have given the interviewer a way to see you in a different light from other candidates.

Reach out to any past managers and tell them you are beginning your professional career; ask if they would be willing to act as a reference "when the time comes," and whether they would be prepared to talk about your reliability, honesty, team spirit, flexibility, work ethic, etc. If they answer positively, ask them what they would be comfortable saying on these topics, and take notes. At the end of the conversation, thank the reference for her time and say you will be in touch when an employer asks you for references.

Even with a first job, references can be requested, so it is useful to get them lined up now. Besides, if someone will speak well of you, perhaps you can get him to write an endorsement for your LinkedIn profile; and who better to help you find work than someone for whom you have already performed well?

If it hasn't come up already, at the very end of the conversation take a minute to tell the reference, briefly, what you are looking for. Don't expect anything, but the strangest people can help shape your professional destiny, as you'll see shortly.

If these references are needed, you will call again and confirm what will be said; if they aren't needed, you will still have given yourself some positive reinforcement about the skills you can bring to any professional job, and this should boost your confidence.

Digital Dirt

Do a Google search of your name—and alternate spellings of your name—and see what comes up.

Alexandra Levit, Author, *Blind Spots, www.alexandralevit.com*

Corporate recruiters, peers, hiring managers, and headhunters are constantly on all social networking sites. A recruiter might find you on LinkedIn, but even if she finds you elsewhere, she is quite likely to check out your LinkedIn profile and dig for more personal information on Facebook. If social networking was part of your up-all-night college days, go back and clean up your digital dirt; those pictures of you projectile vomiting on Spring Break might not represent the professional that you now need to portray in the most desirable light.

Community-Based Networks

Family and Friends

Your family is the most obvious component of your personal network, and also the easiest to misuse. Typically, family members understand next to nothing about what you plan to do for a living, but don't ever discount the value of the members of your family-and-friends networks—they really want to help you, and although many of them still think of you as a snotty ten-year-old, given the right information they can be surprisingly helpful. Case in point: In 1985, my first book was published. Although I've lived here in the States for most of my life, I'm English by birth, and that year I flew home to see my parents for Christmas. My crazy old mother played bridge for years with another crazy old biddy in tweeds and twin sets. I had never taken the old biddy seriously, but that year it turned out she knew someone who owned a publishing company. The result? My first foreign rights sale came from two ladies in their seventies who hadn't ever worked in the professional world, and today, twenty-seven years later, that book is still in print in England. So don't dismiss crazy old Aunt Aggie. She's anxious to help if only you'll show her how—*but without complicating matters with information she doesn't need or understand.*

Even if they have nothing to do with the professional world or have only occasional contact with terrestrials, given the right guidance your immediate family circle and your personal networks can cast a wide net and come up with useful leads. The problem is that it is easy to squander this potentially valuable resource by tapping into it too soon, before you have thought through how best to help your extended family help you.

Here are the steps that make it easier for your loved ones to help you:

1. Think carefully about what you want to do for a living and put it in a one- or two-sentence description that even Aunt Aggie can grasp.
2. Think about the type of company you will work for and the kind of people you need to talk to. Condense this into simple terms and into a one- or two-sentence explanation: "I'm looking for a job with a computer company. It would be great if you or your friends knew anyone who also works with computers." Keep it real simple.
3. Give them the information you need to get in touch with these people: "All I need are the names of people who work with computers. I'm not looking for someone to hire me; I'm just looking to talk to people who also work with computers."

This process of breaking your networking needs into *just three* simple statements gives your immediate circle something they can work with.

The same no-frills approach will work with little change with contacts in your other personal networks.

Civic, Social, Spiritual Associations, and Other Community-Based Networks

Volunteer in your community; gain experience on nonprofit boards or working on special projects for a charitable organization.

Rich Grant, Director of Career Services, *www.thomas.edu*

Your local community is an important source of information, but don't buttonhole people at a first meeting with demands for information about job openings. Spend time getting to know them and become part of the group.

Local networks take more time and effort, but they do result in jobs, and they also involve you in the community at this difficult time of transition into the workforce. If you are prepared to reach out and become part of new groups in your community, not as a kid but as a young professional, it will help you refine your new persona and your personal networking skills, and who knows, you might even get a job lead or two.

Other Community-Based Networks

What can you do to build community-based social networks if you don't belong to a church and haven't played in the same softball league since elementary school? Whatever interests you also interests others, so you can always find a way to connect with like-minded people. While such groups might not have the same value as an alumni or professional association, we all have to work somewhere, so you could meet some professionally relevant people. Try one of the following:

1. Look into Meetup.com. It exists to help people all over the country connect online and meet offline to pursue common interests. There are groups for every interest.
2. Volunteer for any cause that grabs your fancy. Here are some ideas:

- Join the Humane Society. It attracts a wide swathe of the community.
- Become active in the United Way, which supports a wide variety of good causes; visit their website (*www.unitedway.org*) or give them a call and they can put you in touch with a group that resonates.
- Tutor at a community center.
- Start coaching sports.
- Volunteer at food banks and soup kitchens.
- Docent for museums and related ventures.

Join or Create Your Own Job-Search Network

You can also join a local job-search network of your friends and peers or create your own. This can be helpful because job search can be lonely and you will sometimes feel that companies are looking for everyone but you. This isolation can get depressing; you need to be aware of the emotion and learn to manage it, and the most productive way to do this is to join or create a job-search network with other recent grads in your local community. If you need to start one, you could do worse than check out *www.meetup.com.*

The Networking Mindset

Using your network to the best advantage means you've got to get in the right frame of mind. In every conversation or e-mail exchange you have, in every telephone conversation or social gathering, your focus should be on how to grow your networks with the right kinds of people and how to gather useful information from the people with whom you interact *while giving at least as much as you are getting.*

We have touched on finding out what might be of value to each of your contacts and making an effort to pass on information that can have value. But what kinds of questions should you ask of the professionals you meet and interact with during your networking activities? For example, if you know or meet someone who's working for a company you're interested in, you might ask some or all of these questions:

- "What needs does your company have at present?"
- "Who in the company is most likely to need someone with my background?"
- "Who else in the company might need someone with my background?"
- "Do you know if the _____ department is planning any expansion or new projects?"
- "When do you anticipate a change in the company's manpower needs?"
- "Does your company have any other divisions or subsidiaries? Where are they?"
- "Do you know any recruiters who work in this area?"
- "Have you heard of any other companies in the area who might be hiring?"

Be sure to thank the other person for any information he gives you. You should also send a follow-up "thank you" e-mail; this properly expresses your appreciation and keeps your name front and center in his mind.

The quality of help you receive from your network contacts depends on the value you bring to each relationship. While you want answers to the above questions, that doesn't mean they are the first questions you ask. During your job search you will come across information that is of interest to someone else who's looking for a job, and you should capture this information so that you can share it with others and be seen as helpful. You will also come across information that is interesting to people in your profession who are *not* involved in a job search. So, whether they are job hunting or not, try to help everyone you talk to by showing an interest in trying to bring value to their lives. Your concern will help make you a big winner.

There are three steps in using social networking sites to find work, regardless of the tools you use: Positioning, Polishing, and Publishing.

Joshua Waldman, Author, *Job Searching with Social Media for Dummies,* *www.careerenlightenment.com*

RESOURCES Networking letters and resume templates can be found at *www.knock emdead.com.*

You can learn more about networking in *Knock 'em Dead: The Ultimate Job Search Guide,* latest annual edition.

CHAPTER 5

SUCCESSFUL JOB-SEARCH STRATEGIES

In a competitive job market, you cannot rely exclusively on networking or, for that matter, any other single job search tool. I wish I could tell you the one true strategic tool that will find this all-important first job, but the fact is that they all work, and because you never know which one is going to deliver your first step on the ladder of success, you have to use them all. Combine them effectively, as you will learn how to do in this chapter, and you can triple and quadruple your results.

Job Sites

There are so many thousands of job sites that you could never hope to visit them all, and because you don't want to spend an eternity flitting from one job site to the next, you have to intelligently integrate this aspect of your search into your overall strategy. You should begin by researching which sites are most relevant to your search—try Googling "entry-level job sites" and "new graduate job sites." Then try similar searches that focus on your profession; for example, if you used "entry-level tech jobs" as your search phrase, you found plenty of sites and other useful information. When I did this search, a great link to the "ten worst entry-level tech jobs" came up—something well worth knowing. To help you get started try:

www.collegejobbank.com
www.collegerecruiter.com
www.entryleveljobsite.com
www.experience.com

You should also try job site spiders/aggregators such as Indeed .com and SimplyHired.com. These sites accept your search terms— "entry-level accountant," for example—and then search the Internet for job postings.

> Job sites are a great place to spend ten minutes a day finding job leads. Once a lead is found, you are better served by networking via LinkedIn or within your local community for connections within the target company.
>
> **Tim Tyrell-Smith**, Founder, *www.timsstrategy.com*

Your goal is to create a growing database of job sites that generate job postings relevant to your needs. Spend a morning developing a list of potentially interesting job sites and the afternoon visiting them to decide if they are likely to help your job search. Does the site have job postings that are suitable for you? If not, you can move on to the next site. If it does, you will want to register with the site to receive e-mail alerts when new jobs matching your criteria get posted to the site. When you register with a job site, use your resume as the template to create your profile, just as you did on LinkedIn.

When you request e-mail alerts, you will be asked to define the jobs that interest you. When answering this question, keep your parameters wide; it is better to plow through a little junk than miss a great opportunity. Over the next few weeks you can narrow your parameters to get better matches and weed out less relevant jobs. But before you do, remember that those jobs that aren't quite right for you could be just right for your networking contacts; passing on opportunities to contacts is a crucial—and all-too-often overlooked—part of maintaining your network.

When you are asked about relocation and geographical preference in the registration process, leave these issues "open." Why?

- It's better to reject an opportunity than never to hear about it.
- *Your weakest professional survival skill is also the most critical to your professional survival and success: turning job interviews into job offers.* Every opportunity to build skills and experience here should be seized, even if you don't want the job.
- We'd all move to Possum Trot, Kentucky (yes, such a place exists), for the right opportunity and package.

Spelling and punctuation are important. Filling out online forms and applications without proper spelling, capitalization, and punctuation will hurt your chances. Always write your documents in Word, save them, and proof them with the spell-checker before uploading.

As you start out in your professional life, it will seem that employers only want to hire people with a minimum of three years' experience. A few years down the road, when you are looking to make a change, it will seem as if every employer on the planet is looking for entry-level workers. This can be very frustrating unless you develop ways to leverage what appear to be useless job postings.

It is logical that a company hiring other titles, and especially other titles in your department, might also be looking for someone like you *but just not advertising where you happen to be looking*; there are so many thousands of job sites on the Internet that you cannot ever hope to have seen all the job postings for your target job title. The following high-value job titles are always worth watching for when you visit job banks, because job postings for other titles in your immediate area increase the odds of *your* job title being sought by that employer, either now or in the immediate future. Look for these high-value titles:

- The same job title but requiring more experience
- Job titles one to three levels above you
- Other job titles in the same department

You can use postings for these high-value job titles in a number of ways:

1. They identify companies that hire professionals like you.
2. They lead you to a company website where you can read the other listed job postings; if there is a posting for you, respond to it. If not, upload your resume anyway.
3. The job postings for these high-value job titles are exactly the same ones you focus on in your networking activities—the people who would most appreciate knowing about these jobs are the same people most likely to know about jobs for you, and consequently most capable of giving you leads, introductions, and referrals. Pass on these leads, build goodwill, and your contacts will likely return the favor.
4. Even if you see no job postings, if the company fits your employment criteria of being in the industry/profession where you want to work, and also being located within your target location, that company is worth approaching. More on this later.

Googling for Jobs

You can also Google variations of your target job title(s). Most people get bored after the first couple of pages of a Google search, but this part of your search isn't brain surgery and you can drill down thirty or forty pages and still find jobs, job sites, employers, and recruiters while watching the boob tube. You'll come across many jobs that hold no immediate interest, but each of these "irrelevant jobs" is posted on a website that might have a relevant opportunity and/or resources that could be helpful to your networking contacts. Whenever you come across information that could be of interest to you or friends, capture it. In the digital age knowledge, used wisely, makes you influential.

Resume Banks

The job sites you visit also have resume banks, and the recruiters who are posting jobs to those sites are also searching their resume banks. If you find the job postings interesting, you'll want to upload your resume.

In Chapter 3 we discussed creating a resume that is visually accessible to recruiters and hiring managers. However, the formatting of Word documents can cause problems for the ATS software (Applicant Tracking System) used by the resume banks, so you will need to create a Plain Text or ASCII version of your resume to upload into the resume banks. This isn't difficult to do, but it does take a few minutes. The process is explained in *Knock 'em Dead Resumes & Templates,* available only at *www.knockemdead.com.*

You should know that recruiters pay for access to resume banks, so the job sites tend to purge old resumes (usually every ninety days) so that the paying customers can be assured of fresh resumes. This means that you'll need to note the date you posted a resume and mark your calendar to alert you to the need to reload the resume before the ninety-day deadline. Recruiters visit these sites regularly and are usually offered a tool to view resumes *by posting date*, enabling them to restrict their searches to only the most recent resumes. You will probably identify six to ten job sites where you want to remain maximally visible. If you don't want to be overlooked because of the posting date issue, you'll need to go back every week or two to update your resume. How do you do this?

In reading job postings, you will come up with keywords that describe skills not currently listed in your Professional Skills/Core Competency section. Adding these skills not only gives you a meaningful way to update your profile, it refreshes your "posted on" date—the search engines see any change to your document as a new resume being posted.

If you can't come up with any such skills to add, just delete a word from your resume, log off, log on again, and put the word back in place.

Job Fairs

Job fairs are occasions when, usually under the auspices of a college or job fair promoter, employers get together to attract large numbers of potential employees to a one-day-only event. Campus-based job fairs are typically free, while that job fair happening at your local town hall will probably charge a small entrance fee, in return for which you get direct access to all the employers and formal presentations by company representatives and local employment experts. When you organize yourself properly, take the right attitude, and work all the opportunities, job fairs make for a great entry-level job search opportunity.

When you attend job fairs, go prepared with:

- **Proper business attire.** You may be meeting your new boss, and you don't want the first impression to be less than professional.
- **Your resume.** You should take as many copies of your resume as there are exhibitors, times two. You'll need one to leave at the exhibit booth and an additional copy for anyone you have a meaningful conversation with. If you have resumes targeted to different jobs, take copies of all of them.
- **Laptop or notepad and pen**, preferably in a folder.

Job fairs are an opportunity for networking with other job hunters as well. If you know other people going to a job fair, you should go with a collaborative effort in mind. Your friends may well be pursuing entirely different jobs and different professions, but if you all make the effort to speak to other attendees and collect business cards from everyone you meet, regardless of sex, age, job, or profession, together you can generate far more leads.

If you are attending solo, make the effort to network with other attendees and build your network and again suggest you work together. Ask them to meet you later in the day to exchange leads that might be mutually beneficial. I have witnessed this in action at job fairs and seen a group of twenty who were total strangers in the morning happily exchanging information and business cards at the end of the day. Aside from covering more ground at the job fair, you can add substantially to your LinkedIn contacts through such improvised groups.

It's easy to walk into a job fair and be drawn like a moth to the biggest and most attractive booths—sponsored by the largest and most established companies—and ignore the lesser ones. Remember that *companies with less than 500 employees generate the majority of the jobs in America.* Armed with this insight, you will visit every booth, not just the ones with the flashing lights and all the moths fluttering around.

- You can approach and talk to absolutely anyone at a job fair—no one will blow you off. Talk to a representative at every booth; ask questions about company activities, and who they are looking for, before you talk about yourself. You can't know how to sell yourself if you don't know what they want.
- Very few people actually get hired at job fairs; for most companies the exercise is one of collecting resumes so that meaningful meetings can take place in the ensuing days and weeks. Nevertheless, you should be "on" at all times, because serious interviews do sometimes occur on the spot. Collect business cards from everyone you speak to, so you can follow up with an e-mail and a call when they are not so harried.

  If you have a background and resume that match a specific opportunity, make your pitch, but only after you have asked about the job and the company. If, on the other hand, there's a job you can do, but your resume needs some adaptation to better position your candidacy, take a different approach. By all means pitch the company representative, but don't hand over a resume that will detract from your candidacy (you can come up with a harmless pretext, such as having run out of copies). Instead, get the contact's business card and promise to follow up with a resume, which you can then custom-fit to the opportunity (see the *TJD* process in Chapter 3).
- Collect company brochures and collateral materials.

- Arrange times and dates to follow up with as many employers as possible: "Ms. Jones, I realize you are very busy today, but I would like to speak to you further. Your opportunities in _____ sound exactly suited to my education and interests. I would like to set up a time when we could talk."

In addition to the exhibit hall, there will probably be formal group presentations by employers. As all speakers love feedback, move in when the crush of presenter groupies has died down. You will have more knowledge of the company from the exchanges with the people in front of you, and time to customize your pitch to the needs and interests of the employer; besides, you'll get more time and closer attention. Open with a compliment about the person's platform skills: "You are such a good speaker! How long did it take you to develop those skills?" After that, you can usually ask all the questions you want.

On leaving each booth, and again at the end of the day, go through your notes while everything is still fresh in your mind. Review each company and what possibilities it may hold for you. Also review what you have learned about industry trends, new skill requirements, marketplace shifts, and long-term staffing needs. Visit company websites, upload your resume, and send e-mails and make follow-up calls within the week to everyone with whom you spoke.

Internships

> Nine out of ten direct-from-college hires go to those with internship experience. Internships are the most important aspect of early career development.
>
> **Mark Babbitt,** CEO and Founder, *www.youtern.com*

You can pursue internships throughout your college experience and even after graduation. The easiest way to differentiate yourself from your competition is to get some real-world work experience, and the quickest way to do that is with an internship. Working as an intern for a few weeks or months helps you gain professional skills and learn about organizational culture. You will find out what it is like to work in a particular industry, make contacts, and maybe even get job offers.

Employers really like internship programs because it allows them to test-drive potential employees and choose those most suitable to their needs.

Even if your internship doesn't turn into a job offer, you will have gained real-world experience, and that beefs up your resume and helps you appear much more grounded and experienced at job interviews. You will also gain references; just because someone can't hire you doesn't mean they thought you did a crummy job.

> Employers expect to see internships on a resume. It's the ticket to a good entry-level job out of college.
>
> **Rich Grant,** Director of Career Services, *www.thomas.edu*

Paid Versus Unpaid

Both paid and unpaid internships exist. Paid internships are common in commercial and investment banking, venture capital, accounting, and IT. However, the more attractive the profession in terms of entertainment and celebrity, the less the internships are likely to pay, because competition for those internships is so keen. In these instances less pay—or no pay at all—allows employers to weed out all but the serious interns.

Ideally, you want to be paid for your work, but if ever there is a time in your career when you can work for nothing and still come out ahead, it is with an internship that will give you real-world experience and help jump-start your career.

What Job? What Industry? What Sort of Company?

> Quite often, internships lead to full-time employment at the end of your college career, and if you're unsure of the direction you wish to go with your career, multiple internships can give you clarity.
>
> **Sandra Ingemansen, CPRW,** Principal, *www.resume-strategies.com*

Any internship is better than none, but if you have the choice, you should look for opportunities that relate to the job you want, within industries in which you would consider starting your career. E-commerce, for example, is a growing industry, and internships there are likely to lead to contacts and jobs in a growing market sector. On the other hand, if all you can get is an internship in the paper and pulp industry (it's a dying industry in America and moving offshore), while this is probably not a sector to set your sights on for a sustainable career, you would still be gaining experience in a professional workplace and any work experience is better than none.

> Internships can really help you determine what you do and don't want to be doing in your career. If you hate your internship, the odds are good you might hate the job when you're getting paid to do it.
>
> **Josh Tolan,** CEO, *www.sparkhire.com*

When it comes to companies, everyone wants to work for Google or Apple. Great if you can pull it off, but there are also many other great options beyond the household names and *Fortune* 500 companies. You can work on terrific projects and gain valuable experience working for a little-known company as an intern—after all, Google started on a kitchen table in 1997.

How to Find Internships

Internships can now be found 24/7 and year-round. If you have a set deadline for when you would like an internship to start (or stop, given that the average internship is ten to thirteen weeks) start applying at least six weeks ahead of the desired start date.

Mark Babbitt, CEO and Founder, *www.youtern.com*

There are plenty of intern resources on- and off-campus:

- **Career Services Office.** Ask for the internship coordinator.
- **Alumni Association Office.** Colleges increasingly ask alumni to sponsor internships.
- **Major/Minor Department.** Internship programs specific to your major are usually tracked by a faculty member; go to the department's office and ask.
- **Career Fairs.** Campus career fairs feature companies recruiting entry-level employees, but you can also approach the recruiters about internships.
- **Direct to employer.** You can also use direct research and approach techniques (addressed in a few pages) to identify desirable employers in your target location. You can then visit their websites to look for internship opportunities. You can also do a general search on LinkedIn for "college recruiter," or you could add a company name and/or a brand name.
- **Networking.** You can apply all the networking techniques discussed earlier to discover internships, plus career services at your school, your alumni networks, and the alumni office. You can also use Twitter effectively: Try the hashtag "#internships."

Use Twitter hashtags such as #job, #jobsearch, #hiring to find jobs then add #yourcity to see if any jobs are listed in your city. You can also use smartphone apps such as jobcompass to see jobs listed nearby.

Sultan Camp, Military Transition and Social Network Specialist, *www.zeiders.com*

- **Job sites.** While *www.YouTern.com* is the number one site for internships, you should also visit these respected sites:
  www.Idealist.org
  www.internjobs.com
  www.internweb.com
  www.urbaninterns.com
  www.aftercollege.com
  www.externs.com
  www.ihipo.com
  www.internshipking.com
  www.internshipprograms.com
  www.itraineeship.com
- **Job spiders.** Search for internships using job spiders such as Indeed.com and SimplyHired.com.

No Free Lunch in the Professional World

When you see postings for internships, respond as requested, but also remember to cross-reference the company with all your social networks, looking for people you know who work or have worked there. Ask them for referrals to the people handling internships—whenever you can reach out to someone personally, your odds of *getting into conversation*, and therefore of getting an offer, are that much better.

Pursuing internships is an activity similar to job hunting: You have to pursue as many as are relevant to your goals, and you cannot afford to pin your hopes on one particularly attractive opportunity. Internships can disintegrate in front of your eyes just like that dead-certain job offer that never materialized, so follow up on all your internship applications right up till your first day of work. Follow-up is addressed later.

How to Tap Into the Hidden Job Market

Identify the decision-makers for the department or company. Do they want to talk to you? Of course not; they're busy. However, the great salesperson finds the magic words to get the meeting. It takes persistence. It takes confidence. So why do you keep sending resumes to HR? Do they control the budget?

Hannah Morgan, Job Search Strategist, *www.careersherpa.net*

What is meant by "targeting desirable employers"? We all know companies like Apple and Google, and we all know that they get thousands of applications every day; but beyond the household names, how do you find potential employers except by finding their job postings? You have already identified the most obvious potential employers by searching job banks and responding to appropriate job postings. But are the only possible jobs and the only possible employers those you have already seen on the job banks you happen to frequent? Of course not.

Doing your own research using online research tools (often available through your career services department or reference books in your local research library) enables you to identify 99.9 percent of potential employers in any given profession, industry, or geographic area. With this information, you can tap into the hidden job market, finding great employers and jobs that other job hunters will never find because they are not so deeply invested in professional success, and so will not make the effort.

More Jobs and More Employers Are Hiding in Plain Sight

Tapping into this "hidden job market," as it's mysteriously referred to, is actually pretty straightforward. Online and local library–based resources are a valuable supplement to the information you gather about potential employers from job banks, job fairs, and networking. There are many great job-search tools that have been designed for other business uses, for example:

- Standard and Poor's (S & P) (*www.standardandpoors.com*) is a major research tool designed for the financial services industry, but has been a godsend for millions of job-seekers too.

  S & P identifies every publicly traded company in the world and indexes them by industry, location, products and services delivered, and in countless other ways. The information on individual companies is detailed, telling you what the company does, providing contact information, and including a listing of key executives at the VP level and above. They even have a database of executives organized by name, personal information (schools, graduation dates, interests, clubs, etc.), title, and contact information.

- Hoovers.com, a Dun & Bradstreet company, has a website that, while not designed for job-seekers, is perfect for your direct research and approach needs. It identifies over eighty-five million public and private companies along with many other tools.

If you use these research tools along with cross-referenced job postings as described, you will have a complete picture of all the employers in your target location that could possibly need someone with your professional expertise.

You can use all these resources to build an employer and job-search database for your industry/profession/specialty that will help you tap into the hidden job market. And because the statistics say you will change jobs with some regularity over the years, gathering and saving all relevant information on employers you find now will give you better control of your professional destiny when, a few years down the road, you plan your first strategic career move.

RESOURCES You can find much more information on job search tactics in each of these and other areas in *Knock 'em Dead: The Ultimate Job Search Guide* (latest annual edition) and at *www.knockemdead.com* on the job-search advice pages. Cover letter and other job search letter templates are also available on the website.

CHAPTER 6

HOW TO EXECUTE A NETWORK-INTEGRATED JOB SEARCH

Nothing happens in the professional world without conversations taking place, and that holds for your first job search too. Without conversations taking place, interviews don't get scheduled and job offers don't get made. That's why the focus of your job search is, "How do I *get into conversation as quickly and as often as possible with the people who can hire me?*" You can wait for these conversations to happen or you can make them happen. In this chapter, we'll look at how you can integrate professional networking strategies into every aspect of your job search.

> You should spend 90 percent of your time talking to people.
>
> **Caroline Dowd-Higgins,** Career Director, Maurer School of Law; CBS Radio Host, *www.carolinedowdhiggins.com*

Sales and Marketing Strategies

You've posted your resume on resume banks, sent it in response to company job postings, and adapted and developed the content to fit your LinkedIn profile. Every time you send out your resume, it acts like a baited fishhook, and you've baited your hook well. But just sitting back and waiting for a bite isn't the way to land your first job.

Like it or not, your job search is a sales and marketing job. Jobs in sales exist to generate revenue by getting into conversation with customers and selling them the product; they exist because marketing alone—positioning the product in a flattering light and in places where potential buyers will see it—is never enough for consistent profitability.

Remember the Introduction, where we first discussed thinking of yourself as a financial entity—as MeInc—a corporation that must survive through generating sales? For MeInc, sales means getting into conversations that lead to interviews and job offers. Your successful job search, like any sales campaign, depends on your *getting into conversations, as quickly and as often as possible, with people who can make the decision to hire you.*

Who to Approach Within Your Target Companies

The recent grads who break away from the pack are the ones who take that extra step, who are committed to steering the ship rather than being tugged by the eddies and flows of a volatile market. This means doing more than just responding to job postings and uploading your resume to resume banks. If you are one of these people, you will have taken the advice of this book and identified every company within the geographic boundaries of your job search who could possibly hire someone like you. If so, I congratulate you on sticking to the plan—your dedication will pay off. But companies aren't enough; you need to find *people* within those companies to talk to.

> Online job boards can be a great resource for leads inside companies. But networking and leveraging relationships (online and offline) allows you to move beyond a piece of paper and toward a more personal connection that, more often than not, is the reason you get hired.
>
> **Kevin Kermes,** Founder, *www.careerattraction.com*

Again and again we've had occasion to recall this basic fact of career strategy: *Getting into conversation with the people who have the authority to hire you* is the central goal of all your job search tactics.

It is also the activity that every entry-level job hunter like you most wants to ignore, because talking to strangers seems like a scary thing to do.

It's not scary. You do it all the time.

Your first step is to identify who you want to talk to and how you are going to find them. The people you want to *talk to as quickly and often as possible* are:

- People holding those job titles most likely to have the authority to offer you a job.
- Corporate recruiters and college recruiters.
- People who hold the same job title you want to get—because when you are starting out *everyone* has more experience and you are not a threat. These people will have jobs in the departments where you might like to work, and will know the high-value job titles one to three levels above you.

High-Value Networking Assets

Put these titles together and you have a hotlist of the high-value job titles that represent people who are most likely to know about suitable jobs for you and who are in a position to hire you or make the right introductions to someone who can. These are the people you want to *get into conversation with as quickly and as often as possible.*

Of slightly lesser value, but worth looking out for, are people who hold job titles one to three levels above your own outside your department, but in departments that have regular contact with your target department.

> Developing networking relationships with the above titles can have a decisive effect on this and all future job searches. These are your professional colleagues, and for as long as you are in this profession, they will be the people who can help you most. Initiate conversations; build relationships by bringing value.
>
> **Joshua Waldman,** Author, *Job Searching with Social Media for Dummies,* www.careerenlightenment.com

Professional relationships thrive on reciprocity, so just as you hope for help with the things you need, you must also be prepared to help your colleagues whenever the opportunity arises. Since these job titles also represent the titles of job postings you will stumble across and have no use for during almost every day of your job search, you can save them and:

- Whenever you are "talking" (e-mail/text/phone) with a target title, you have something of potential value that you can casually and gracefully offer.
- On a daily basis, via your LinkedIn, Facebook, and Twitter feeds, you can announce what you have found: "Have a lead on a great job for an Accounting Manager. Know anyone? Pass it on." On a weekly basis you could make a short list, "This week, stumbled on great jobs for 4 senior accountants and 3 accounting managers. All in Minnesota."

The challenge, of course, is building strong networks where these and similar titles are predominant.

How to Find High-Value Networking Contacts

You can find these people through your social networks. Using LinkedIn as a reference and our trusty "Accountant" as an example, you can join groups relevant to your profession and:

- Search the membership list for these titles, check out the profiles, and request a connection based on a shared profession and group.
- Make complimentary comments on posts of people who are your professional seniors, and subsequently ask them to connect.
- Ask your own questions, as we have discussed; then connect with the people who comment.

You can also search the LinkedIn database by job title and location; for example: "Accountant Boston." Then check the profile to see if you have mutual connections that can justify your connection request. At the beginning of your career, the best bet is to look for mutual group membership, because this allows you to reach out to anyone.

You might be asking the question, "Who wants to connect with someone like me?" Plenty of people. Professionals have always known that strong networks are a great job-search and career-management tool, yet before social networking and LinkedIn, few people had the time to build truly useful networks. The people who join LinkedIn are people who have awoken to the fact that deep and relevant networks are not only desirable, but also possible.

With direct research you are able to identify companies of interest in your target location. Now you can get a second use out of those company names by cross-referencing for contacts on LinkedIn and your other professional networking profiles. Look for these employers—and for your identified high-value networking titles— in the special interest groups you belong to. Search in one of your groups with a phrase relevant to your job hunt, for example: "V.P. Finance Calabrese, Inc., IL." Then, using a cross-section of your different network connections, LinkedIn group memberships, or introductions through existing contacts, you can reach out to make a connection.

Six degrees of Kevin Bacon. Most people are connected in some fashion, through social networking sites, churches, or your mother's friend's son.

Mike Squires, Senior Technical Recruiter, PayPal, *www.paypal.com*

Searching for High-Value Titles at Target Companies

You can also use the search engine(s) of your choice to find the names of high-value contacts at particular companies. For example, Google: "Pharmaceutical sales [*company name*] Pennsylvania." Then make the same search adding words like "sales," "hiring manager," "VP sales," or the city (say, "Pittsburgh").

Yes, going through all these permutations takes a little work, but this is your future calling; and besides, you can do these searches while watching TV.

As you complete each search using a potential hiring title, repeat that search as a Google News search. These searches look for mentions of your keywords in media coverage. Leave your search terms in the dialogue box and simply hit the **News** tab above on the navigation bar.

Doing news searches has multiple benefits:

- You can find names and titles
- Because they come in the context of a story, you have a conversational icebreaker for your e-mail or conversation. Copy an interesting, relevant article and attach it in an e-mail. With a traditional letter, enclose a copy of the article. In both, your letter will open with mention of the media coverage, and this alone, through the immutable laws of ego, guarantees that the rest of your message will be read. It is even more effective when you use it to open a telephone conversation: "I've been meaning to call you ever since I saw the article in _____."
- Interesting articles about your profession also offer good material to post on your social networking groups and on LinkedIn/Facebook/Twitter feeds. It shows you are engaged—which is appealing to recruiters—and because you are sharing items of potential interest to others in your profession, it positions you as a sphere of influence.
- In standard and news searches with Google, Bing, etc., you will also unearth job postings.
- Standard and news searches with Google and Bing, etc., will also unearth headhunters with job postings above your experience level. Capturing such postings is crucial for the oft-ignored *quid pro quo* (literally "this for that," and a phrase often used in the corporate world referring to giving as much as you take) part of your networking activities.

- Headhunters are typically not interested in entry-level people, but you can make inroads with a polite e-mail explaining that you understand this fact, but are making lots of contacts with people the headhunter *is* looking for, and would be happy to pass these contacts on. Unspoken is the fact that the headhunter will give you some advice and/or direction. If you do this, and offer, say, four names, you might be in a position to ask the headhunter for reciprocal information about four companies that could help you. There won't be a direct *quid pro quo*, but if you have questions to ask, there's a greater likelihood of their being answered.

By using these direct research approaches, you are able to identify the exact people and employers who will lead to your entry into the professional world. You will know who you need to talk to and why and, by sharing useful information and leads on professional opportunities, you will often have some of the means of contributing to the relationship. Your irrational fear of talking to strangers won't disappear, but it will dissipate: for you are in fact making a serious professional contribution with—believe it or not—your *colleagues*.

Capture Information

Capture the information you gather so that you can access and use it in this job search, and perhaps for other job searches down the road. If you stay in this profession and location, most of the companies and many of the same people will still be there next time you're looking for a job. They're still going to be putting out the same product, and they're still going to be hiring people like you. It's easy to ignore this sort of long-term thinking when you're desperate just to get your foot in the door, but you came to this book because you care about building a successful and rewarding career, and that requires laying the foundations now for relationships that may not pay off for years to come. Direct research, integrated with intelligent networking strategy, helps you become knowledgeable about your industry and connects you to the people who make up the core of your profession.

How do you get a foothold in the hidden job market? Compile a list of ten to twenty target companies that are a good fit. Find one or two key people within each company. Connect with your key people through cold contact, an introduction, social networks, and/or other networking methods.

Meg Guiseppi, C-level Executive Job-Search Coach, *www.executivecareerbrand.com*

Beware Dream Employers

As you gather information about individual companies in your target area, one or more of them will emerge as dream employers. Resist the urge to apply for jobs with these "super-desirable" employers right away. Your resume and interviewing skills are not yet up to speed at the beginning of your first professional job search; the last thing you need is to fumble an opportunity to join the company of your dreams. It is better to hold off until you know that your resume is fine-tuned and that you won't swallow your tongue in the first few minutes of the interview. Then, when you feel confident, use network contacts to get insider information and referrals, and your approach to that dream employer is likely to be a smoother experience.

How to Quadruple Your Chances of an Interview

The more ways you approach your target companies and hiring managers, the faster you will *get into conversation with the people who can and will hire you.* Let's say you respond to a job posting by uploading your resume; this action gives you just one chance of getting an interview.

You can quadruple your chances of an interview if you also:

1. E-mail your resume directly to the manager by name with a personalized cover letter. This alone will double your chances of an interview.

2. Before you were born, people of my generation used to send something called letters. We would put them in folded pieces of paper called envelopes and deposit them at a building called the post office, where nice ladies and men in blue would take them and deliver them to anyone we asked.

   This may seem barbaric to you, but sending a resume and personalized cover letter to a manager by traditional mail will triple your chances of an interview. We all like a break from the computer screen, so delivering your sales message and resume this way can be very effective.

   When you do this, note in the cover letter that you sent the resume by e-mail and that you're making this additional approach because you are really interested in the company and "wanted to increase my chances of getting your attention." This will triple your chances of an interview.

3. Make a follow-up telephone call to that manager first thing in the morning, at lunchtime, or at 5:00 P.M. (when she is most likely to be available, unprotected by gatekeepers, and picking up her own phone), and you will quadruple your chances of an interview.

Remember, a successful job search is all about *getting into conversation as quickly and as often as possible with people in a position to hire you.* The more frequently you get into conversation with the high-value job titles that matter in your job search, the faster you will land that new position, because:

- You have skipped right over the hurdle of your resume being found and pulled from the commercial resume database.
- You have sidestepped the corporate recruiter's evaluation process.
- You have the attention of someone who either has the authority to hire you or is intimately involved with that person on a daily basis.
- You have earned the opportunity to open one of those *all-important* personal conversations and make a direct and personal pitch.

Getting a resume to someone by name with a personalized pitch gives you a distinct advantage, never more important than when the economy is down or in recovery and when you're looking to get your foot on that first rung of the professional ladder. At such times your competition is fierce and employers really do recognize and appreciate the initiative and *motivation* you display by doing these things, especially picking up the phone and calling. Think about it: Most of your competition will be equally young and inexperienced, and your confidence and poise in putting yourself out there will speak to your determination and *emotional maturity*. This makes you stand out.

Initiating Conversation with Recruiters and Hiring Managers

Talking to the people with high-value titles who haven't seen your resume, and following up on resumes you send out with a phone call, is the best way to get the job interviews that will lead to job offers and the launch of your career. Picking up your telephone and talking to the right people is one of the best tactics available for getting job interviews.

During a day's job-search work, you will upload your resume to resume databases and send it to the high-value contacts you identified; during the same daily job-search activities, you should always make a few minutes to pick up the phone and introduce yourself to those high-value job titles that you identified and approached with a resume a day or two ago. Whenever you send an e-mail or traditional letter pitching your resume, you should follow it up a couple of days later with a telephone call. The more often these conversations happen, the more quickly your search will end in success, and this step is never more important than when the economy is in flux and jobs are harder to find.

How to Make Successful Phone Calls

Don't deceive yourself by thinking this part of the search is not possible because you are terrified of picking up the phone to call strangers. We all talk on the phone all the time—these are just calls with a special purpose. It is something you can learn to do successfully, and whatever small pain it causes is far outweighed by what you gain: a new job and some experience in successful career management.

If you have just a single goal when you pick up the phone—get an interview—you have just one chance of success but many more of failure. But if you have multiple goals for your call, you have multiple chances for success. When headhunters make sales/marketing calls, they usually have four commonsense goals in mind. You can adapt them to fit your needs in launching your professional career.

1. I will arrange an interview date and time.
2. If my contact is busy, I will arrange another time to talk.
3. If I can't get an interview, I will develop leads on other job openings.
4. I will leave the door open to talk with this person again in the future.

Keep these goals in mind every time you talk with someone during your job search, because every conversation holds the potential for turning into an interview or leading you toward another conversation that will generate first a phone conversation and then a face-to-face meeting.

You might worry about calling people directly because you are concerned that they will be annoyed by the perceived intrusion. This is a misconception: The first job of any manager is to get work done through others, so every smart manager is always on the lookout for talent, if not for today, then for tomorrow. If that isn't enough to allay your fears, keep in mind that the person on the other end of the line once upon a time had to find her first job too and is therefore sympathetic to your situation. If you can be concise and professional, you'll find that the great majority of people you contact will try to be helpful.

Paint a Word-Picture

The secret is to be succinct. With an initial introduction and presentation that comes in at well under a minute, you won't be construed as wasting anybody's time. Your aim is to paint a picture of your skills with the widest appeal while keeping it brief—out of courtesy, but also to avoid giving information that might rule you out.

Step #1

Give the employer a snapshot of who you are and what you can do. The intent is to give that person a reason to stay on the phone. You may sometimes have an introduction from a networking colleague, in which case you will build a bridge with that:

"Miss Shepburn? Good morning, my name is Martin Yate, and our mutual friend Greg Spencer suggested I call. Greg says 'hello' by the way . . ."

Or you may have gotten the name and contact information from, for example, a professional association database, in which case you will use that as a bridge:

"Miss Shepburn? My name is Martin Yate. We haven't spoken before, but as we are both members of the _____ association, I hoped I might get a couple of minutes of your time for some advice . . . Is now a good time to talk?"

Asking whether you have caught someone at a good time will get a positive response more often than asking "Have I caught you at a bad time?"

Step #2

You don't want to waste anyone's time by stuttering or *uhmming* and *ahhhing* like a schoolboy. You may be a little nervous, but you can do this. Your goal is to capture a picture of what the *professional you* can offer in less than forty-five seconds. The good news is that you already have the text for what you need to say.

In creating your resume, you completed *TJD* exercises that helped you prioritize employers' needs for your job title. Then, when you wrote the Performance Summary/Profile for your resume, you condensed those employer priorities into three or four short sentences. Consequently, you already know what aspects of your skills and education have the widest appeal, and all you have to do is retool them for speaking rather than reading.

To create a spoken version, take the sentences and turn them into bullet points so that you can recite them word for word, even if you sound like you're reading a script.

Once you have a script, speak it aloud a few times until it sounds conversational and relaxed. Do it in a normal speaking voice until you are comfortable with the content and the rhythm. You can also practice it with a friend or record yourself and listen to the playbacks.

After your introduction you pause for agreement and then add the three or four sentences of summary. For example, an accounting/finance graduate might say:

"I'm a recent Accounting graduate. I worked twenty hours a week while attending college full-time and as a result I already have exposure to the workplace and some basic professional skills."

Or an environmental science graduate might say, "I just graduated with BA in Geography. I don't have experience yet, but I have multiple certifications covering a full range of skills related to GIS, environmental safety, and rescue measures. In my internship I gained experience coordinating with clients, city planning departments, and subcontractors during planning and building phases of projects."

An engineer with only college coursework to rely on might say, "I have a BS in biomedical engineering, strong statistical analysis abilities, and solid analytical skills combined with initiative, technical writing skills, and documentation capabilities. I'm familiar with ISO 9001 and 21 CFR 820, and I'm bilingual."

Step #3
Having introduced yourself professionally and succinctly, get to the reason for your call and move the conversation forward.

"The reason I'm calling is that I'm eager to start my career with a manager who can put me to work developing these skills. Are these the types of skills you look for in entry-level associates?"

Notice that your presentation finishes not with, "Have you got a job? Can you hire me?" but with a question that encourages a response that opens conversation and perhaps gives you some useful information.

When you make your presentation for real, there will often be a short silence on the other end of the line while the recruiter evaluates your pitch. Be patient; you asked a reasonable question, now give your listener a reasonable chance to think.

Conversation is a two-way street, and you are most likely to win an interview when you take responsibility for your half. Just as the employer's questions show interest in you, your questions should show your interest in the work done at the company. By asking questions of your own in the normal course of conversation—questions usually tagged on to the end of one of your answers—you will forward the conversation. Whatever the voice on the other end of the line says next, try to give short, reasonable answers, and finish your reply with a question whenever it makes sense to do so.

When the employer does respond, it will either be with a question—denoting interest—or with an objection. Here's an example of how such a conversation might proceed. Because you and I come from different backgrounds, we will never speak alike, so with the following example, focus on the essence of what is being said, rather than the exact words I am using: You can tailor these suggestions to your own speech patterns.

You have just said something along the lines of, *"The reason I'm calling is that I'm eager to start my career with a manager who can put me to work developing these skills. Are these the types of skills you look for in entry-level associates?"*

Any question a recruiter or hiring manager asks shows a degree of interest (in sales, questions are known as "buy signals").

After a pause, the voice on the other end of the line says, *"Yes, they are. Why are you approaching our company?"* [Buy signal!]

The Internet has made research so fast and painless that employers will expect you to know something about them. If a company is worth sending a resume to and then worth calling, you should always invest a few minutes researching what they do.

"What is your degree in?" [Buy signal!]

When your degree relates to the job, as it should, you answer the question and add something new about your understanding of the job, perhaps saying, *"I have an accounting degree. I've always been good at math and I have an analytical turn of mind, so the challenges posed by accounting in the corporate world seemed like a fascinating and natural choice for me. The accounting function is the engine that helps any company run, and I want to be part of that process."*

Two of the most common buy signals that come up are:

- *"Do you have any work experience?"* If you have experience, answer with the details, emphasizing what you learned that could apply to this job. If you were smart enough to get career-related work during your college years, you are ahead of the game. But even if you only had a fast-food job, you can still apply the lessons learned.

  "I mainly had fast-food jobs working through school, but I still learned a lot. It taught me about punctuality, reliability, dealing with customers, about how to listen and empathize, and about teamwork."

  Then finish with an upbeat, *"I also got promoted, so I learned that if you do a good job, no matter how humble, it is the path to something better. Oh, and I learned I never want to work around french fries ever again."*

- *"What are you looking for?"* While this is an impossible question to answer when you have no frame of reference, it does get asked with some frequency. Your best answer is to come armed with information (from research and your networking conversations) about what everyday life is like in an entry-level job for your target profession (it is going to be grunt work of some description). Your answer will recognize this, yet still show enthusiasm, *"I know I have to start at the bottom, but I'm looking for the opportunity to learn. If you need an entry-level _____, I have the degree and I'm a candidate who knows what I want. If you can give me the opportunity to learn this profession from the ground up, I will do whatever it takes to get the job done."*

- *"How much money do you want?"* As an entry-level candidate, you probably won't face this question at this point—there is very little negotiation for entry-level salaries. If you do get asked this question, say that what you are most interested in is the opportunity to do the work and gain experience, and that you know there is an approved salary range for the position, that that will be acceptable, and that the job and the opportunity to learn the profession and grow is your only goal right now.

Once you hear that second buy signal, it is time to start thinking about asking for a meeting. However, not every call you make will go this smoothly.

Live Leads from Dead Ends

Do not give up. Do not drop out. Do not revert to filling your time all day with Facebook postings or video-game playing. Keep constant pressure on yourself to seek out opportunities and one will come your way. Eventually everyone who keeps at it gets a job.

Dr. Larry Chiagouris, Mentor, *www.thesecrettogettingajobaftercollege.com*

By no means will every hiring manager you call have a job opening that fits your skills, but you can still turn calls that don't result in interviews into successes. Just a couple of pages back we established that your calls have multiple goals, the two most important of which were to: arrange an interview and to develop leads on job openings elsewhere. If there isn't a need for someone like you right now, you can still make the call a success by asking:

- "When do you anticipate new needs in your area?"
- "May I send you my resume and keep in touch for when the situation changes?"
- "Who else in the company might have a need for an entry-level _____?"
- "Do you know who I could speak to about internship opportunities?"

- "What other companies can you think of that might have a need for someone with my background?"

If the response is positive:

- "Thanks, I appreciate the help. Do you know who I should speak to?"

If the response to *that* is positive:

- "May I mention your name?"

You can also mention a company you plan to call:

- "Do you know anyone I could speak to at _____?"

If you ask just this sequence of questions, you will get leads and introductions, and this enables you to open that next call with:

"Hello, Mr. Jones? My name is Martin Yate. Chuck Harris gave me your name and said to tell you hello . . ."

Dealing with Fear

The adrenaline rush you experience when picking up the phone to make the first of these calls is something we associate with fear, and *is normal for anyone engaged in a high-performance activity.* It is a very natural reaction. Even when you know the product you are selling inside out and know exactly what you are going to say and how you are going to say it, I'd be surprised if you weren't still a little leery at the prospect of calling prospective employers. Three pieces of advice always helped me in my hour of need, and I know they will help you too:

- I knew I would never meet these people unless they were interested in what I had to offer, in which case they'd be happy I called.
- Because I was on the phone, no one would know who I was or how scared I felt and looked.

- I knew I had a plan and knew how to make almost every call successful. Even if this person had no need for me, he would be happy to give me a lead . . . if only to get me off the line, or because he could remember what it was like to start out in the work world.

You Have What It Takes to Be Successful

When you structure your calls to hiring managers and recruiters in this way, they will be short, to the point, and entirely professional. And because the person on the other end was once a first-time job seeker too, you will find that the overwhelming majority of people will try to be helpful if you show them a way to do so.

By preparing a sequence of questions that look for opportunities elsewhere, you will achieve a measure of success from every call you make. This will lead to interviews being arranged, and, after a moment of elation at getting your first interview, you can start worrying about how on earth you are going to get through it.

> Go slow to go fast! Get clear on what you want to do that employers will be willing to pay you for. Research your role and field to understand industry trends and choose the employers you'd like to work for. Develop your talking points for networking and job interviews. Network and conduct informational interviews with professionals in your field who can and will help you.
>
> **Phyllis Mufson,** Career Coach, *www.phyllismufson.com*

RESOURCES For more on networking, see *Knock 'em Dead: The Ultimate Job Search Guide*, current annual edition.

See also *Knock 'em Dead Cover Letters*, most recent edition.

For job search letter templates and advice go to *www.knockemdead.com*.

PART III
THE INTERVIEW

CHAPTER 7

Prepare to Turn Your Job Interviews Into Job Offers

In the time you have between arranging the job interview and sitting down to answer the first question, you have to become the *professional persona* that you have taken the time and effort to capture in your resume.

> If you have the opportunity to reach out for informational interviews ahead of time, this can be a priceless opportunity to learn about the company and culture, as well as identify potential contacts you can refer to in your interview—signaling that you did your homework.
>
> **Chris Perry,** Brand and Marketing Generator, *www.careerrocketeer.com*

Divide your time on a two-to-one ratio. For every hour you spend on the mechanics of preparation—researching the company, your route, and means of travel, preparing your wardrobe, etc.—spend two hours with your resume preparing for questions. So if it takes two hours to research the company, invest four hours in reviewing everything that went into your resume; if it takes two hours to get your wardrobe together, invest at least four hours in reviewing how you will respond to interview questions. By the time you arrive at the interview, you should *know the stories that go with every line in your resume*.

You should know how each prioritized responsibility of the job (*TJD*) translates into everyday tasks. Make time to talk with networking contacts and post questions on LinkedIn groups: "I'm a recent grad and have my first interview for a _____ job on Friday. When the employer says they need good analytical skills, how am I likely to be using them on a day-to-day basis?"

The answers you receive will help you understand the *problems your job exists to anticipate, prevent, and solve*, and what you will need to do to shine.

This means you need to:

- Take the time to immerse yourself in each of the job's itemized responsibilities, researching that aspect of the job and asking your network contacts what it takes to do this aspect of the job well.
- With each itemized responsibility, consider the specific *transferable skills* and *professional values* that will help you execute that aspect of the job. Remember, since these professional development projects must take the place of workplace experience until you actually get a job, you need to start honing your *transferable skills **now***.

Go through the job description for this job and your *TJD* repeatedly, comparing the required skills with the story told in your resume until you can relate *any* item or comment in your *TJD* and your resume to *any* item or comment in the job description. You'll know why each responsibility exists and what it takes to do it well.

The Five Secrets of the Hire

There are five secrets to acing a job interview. Understanding them will help you distinguish yourself from other candidates and turn job interviews into job offers. They will also show you how to make a success of your professional life.

1. **Ability and Suitability:** You establish your *ability* to do the job by showing your firm grasp of the *technical skills* of the profession; you exhibit *suitability* for the work in your appearance, demeanor, and the sense of natural professionalism.

2. **Every Job Is about Problem-Solving:** We've discussed this before, but remind yourself of it one last time before walking into that interview: Every job is about *identifying, preventing, and solving problems.* Show that you understand how this applies to your target job and managers will weep with relief and joy.

3. **Professionals Are Professional Because They Behave That Way:** You need to cultivate a *professional persona* that combines the *transferable skills* and *professional values* into an appealing and enthusiastic whole. This will set you apart from all the other recent graduates and set you on track to reach the inner circles of your professional world.

4. **Motivation and Intelligent Enthusiasm:** Show that you understand the work and that you're *intelligently enthusiastic* about doing well, and you will set yourself apart from other candidates.

5. **Teamwork and Manageability:** Every job requires you to work as part of a team toward a greater goal, so you must show that you can be a *team player. Manageability* is the different but related ability to take direction and criticism, even if it's not given with sufficient consideration to your delicate feelings. You take direction and criticism in the right spirit because you care about helping the team reach goals that are impossible through individual effort alone.

When you embrace and apply the five secrets, you will win job offers; and when you apply them on your new job, they will increase your credibility, increase the speed of your acceptance by management and peers, and support your professional growth goals—a conversation that we'll continue.

You can find a much more in-depth discussion of these five secrets on the *Secrets & Strategies for First-Time Job Seekers* page at *www.knockemdead.com.*

Company Research

> You aren't expected to know company financials for the last five years, but you need to know enough to ask good questions.
>
> **Jessica Hernandez,** President, *www.greatresumesfast.com*

The interviewer will expect you to know something about the company's operations, and doesn't expect to spend a lot of time explaining to you what the organization does or how it's positioned in the industry. If you cannot answer convincingly, it will demonstrate a lack of sincere interest, and you will compare poorly against other candidates who make an effort to research the company.

Discover what you can about the position the company occupies within its industry. Is it a leader? Is it growing? How are its products/services distributed? How do these products/services compare to its competitors in terms of functionality, pricing, and availability? If you have done your research, it will show your sincerity and enable you to ask intelligent questions. You should know:

- What the company does, its locations and subsidiaries
- Its current product line and any new products
- News about the company, its products, and key executives
- Its competitors in the industry and in the local market
- Its competitive edge in the market

To gather this information, visit the company website and Google the company name, brands, products, and/or services, along with the names of any interviewers or other company executives of whom you are aware. Having done this, Google News–search the same terms to track media coverage of the company.

If you aren't researching your interviewers, you're lowering your chances for a successful interview. By the way, they're probably looking you up on Google or LinkedIn too!

Joshua Waldman, Author, *Job Searching with Social Media for Dummies,* *www.careerenlightenment.com*

You can also search your existing networks and social networking sites and talk with people who work, or have worked, at this company. Learning that you have an upcoming interview will encourage most people to give you any insights they can. At the same time, if you know any interviewers' names, search these same social networking sites for their profiles; you won't always find anything, but when you do, it's a nice bonus.

Your Interview Kit

Put together an interview kit, and when this interview is over immediately clean and reassemble it in anticipation for the next interview—you never know when it will occur, and you need to be prepared. Your kit will include all the things you'll need to take with you, such as:

- **Printed copies of your resume.** With electronic resumes now the norm, you want to be sure your interviewers see you in the best possible light, and that is in the layout of the print version of your resume. Take half a dozen copies, so that anyone you meet can have a copy to review. You'll also need a copy for yourself so you can refer to it throughout the interview just as the interviewer refers to it. With everything you have to remember, it can be a very useful frame of reference, *recalling not only what is on the page, but also all the thinking that went into creating it.* It is acceptable to look at your resume when interviewers refer to their copies, but you shouldn't look at it after a question asking for, say, dates of employment, because this could imply you don't remember, and some interviewers will question this.

- **A folder with a pad of paper and pen.** Taking occasional notes shows the interviewer that you're paying attention and that you're organized. I don't recommend a PDA, partly because it has too many other potential distractions, but mostly because countless studies have shown that recruiters and hiring managers find them distracting.
- **References.** Take any reference letters you have, although they might not be needed and you shouldn't offer them unless asked.

> An interview is like a first date. You are both looking for a good fit. Focus on the job, be personable, and relax. When you go in desperate and nervous everyone gets turned off and there is no second date.
>
> **Scott Keenan,** HR Generalist, *www.educatedandinexperienced.blogspot.com*

- **A list of job-related questions.** It's good to ask questions during an interview. It shows you're engaged in the discussion and are trying to find out more about how you can integrate yourself into the department and the company. See Chapter 11 to craft the list of questions that is right for you.
- If your research generated any **interesting articles**, print them out and take them along. They indicate your seriousness in researching the company, and sharing them with an interviewer puts the physical proof in her hands.
- **A hairbrush or comb.**
- **A spare pair of tights** (you can skip this item if you're a guy).
- **Bottled water.**
- **Directions to the interview**, including different means of transportation and a timeframe for travel. Nothing is worse than getting lost and being late to a job interview. Long before you depart— you should *never* leave this till the last minute—determine the interview location (building floor, street address, telephone numbers), what transportation you'll use, and the time needed for travel. Murphy's Law tells you that everything that can go wrong

will go wrong on such an important day, so anticipate this and allow plenty of extra time for traffic delays. Getting to the location with *plenty of time to spare* is the only way you can guarantee showing up to the interview calm, ready for battle, and right on time.

> It is essential that you do a practice run at the approximate time the interview is scheduled for, to assess traffic, parking, etc. You should also do a practice interview with someone who has hired people before to get feedback on your performance.
>
> **Sultan Camp,** Military Transition and Social Network Specialist, *www.zeiders.com*

Dress and Grooming

There is a wide range of acceptable dress for the professional workplace. However, even if a company is relatively casual in its everyday dress code, your appearance needs to show that you understand how to dress professionally. It shows that you know what to wear when representing the company and respect the occasion and the interviewer. Dress and grooming are key to interview success, and a misstep here can torpedo your candidacy, but we don't have the space to address them in this book. You can find a discussion of these issues on the *Secrets & Strategies for First-Time Job Seekers* page at *www.knockemdead.com*, and the sartorially challenged can get the full treatment in the latest annual edition of *Knock 'em Dead: The Ultimate Job Search Guide*.

First Impressions

> Breathe, baby, breathe! Do a mock interview with a trusted friend or advisor. Practice makes perfect, and you want to keep it conversational—not too stiff.
>
> **Caroline Dowd-Higgins,** Career Director, Maurer School of Law; CBS Radio Host, *www.carolinedowdhiggins.com*

First impressions are important, and saying or doing the wrong thing can cost you an opportunity. Fortunately, it is fairly easy to avoid making a bad impression and get your interview off to a good start.

The interview begins when you first meet the interviewer. The key to success here is *body language*. It is said that more than half of all effective communication depends on *body language*, because it's our oldest form of communication, and carries enormous weight in the subconscious.

> Shoulders back, chin up, abundant eye contact, a smile and a firm handshake. Few interviewees walk in with this attitude, so recruiters are used to interviews getting off to a bad start. You could surprise the heck out of them.
>
> **Mark Babbitt,** CEO and Founder, *www.youtern.com*

Shake Hands

Let the interviewer initiate the handshake. Match the pressure and style of his shake; it's brief: maybe one to two seconds. At the end of the interview, the handshake will often be repeated in parting. Again, mirror your interviewer's lead.

Personal Space

Whether standing or sitting, we all have a personal space that it is wisest not to invade. A thirty-inch zone surrounding the other person is widely perceived to be everyone's comfort zone. Stay standing until you're invited to sit.

When standing: Keep your posture erect; don't put your hands in your pockets, and don't hook your fingers into your belt.

When sitting: Once you've been offered a seat, avoid nervous fiddling. That's why it's a good idea to take a folder and pen. Keep your butt and back against the back of the chair: It keeps you looking alert and helps you avoid slouching, something many people do when they are feeling nervous.

Look at the Interviewer

During the interview you want to show that you're interested in what's being said. Look at the interviewer while she is talking. You should smile or nod from time to time to show that you understand and are interested in what is being said; you can also make the occasional appreciative murmur to communicate the same thing. Remember to smile: When you are nervous this is easy to forget, but your smile shows friendliness and engagement in what is being said.

> You will command more respect and achieve your desired ends if you are able to dress, act, react, and speak appropriately for your surroundings. Understand that each company, industry, geographic area of the country, and interviewer has its own unique personality, style, preferences, culture, and environment.
>
> **Tegan Acree**, Founder, *www.hiringforhope.org*

Keeping Up Your End of the Conversation

There are a number of techniques you can use to keep up your end of the conversation during a job interview: tactics to clarify questions, buy time to think, and ask useful questions of your own.

1. You can show engagement with what the interviewer is saying by giving verbal signals; you do this with occasional short, quiet interjections that don't interrupt the employer's flow but let her know you are paying attention: "uh-huh," "that's interesting," "okay," "great," and "yes, yes" all work; but be careful not to overdo it.

2. Ask for the question to be repeated, but remember that if you do this more than a couple of times in an interview it can backfire, perhaps making the interviewer think you are a bit slow.

3. When you want to make a point and the interviewer isn't asking questions that allow you to make it, ask questions like these, "Would it be of value if I described my experience at an internship with _____?" or "I had a similar experience at

college in _____, would it be helpful for me to tell you about it?" or "I recently completed a project just like that at school. Would it be relevant to discuss it?"

4. If you still can't answer, say: "I'm sorry, I'm new to interviewing and I'm a little nervous. Can we come back to this question later?" This is perfectly acceptable, and odds are the interviewer will forget to come back to it. If she does ask again later, at least your mind will have been working in the background. If she doesn't but you come up with something good, you can bring it up again yourself. Failing this, you can formulate a good response after the interview and use it as content for a follow-up e-mail: "When we met, you asked me about _____. I was nervous and drew a blank, but of course the minute I got home it hit me: _____."

Conversation Etiquette

Job interviews aren't like casual conversations. Speak clearly and be careful not to mumble or shout, either of which can happen when you are nervous. *Never* interrupt: You want all the information on offer before opening your mouth.

The interviewer wants you to do most of the talking, but you'll want to keep your conversation on-point. As a rule of thumb, you can give a comprehensive answer to most questions in ninety seconds to two minutes. Keep eye contact, and if you feel yourself going over the two-minute mark, look for a signal to continue from the interviewer, or ask, "Would you like me to continue?"

Now that you understand the mechanics, it's time to look at the fifty-nine interview questions you are most likely to face, what's behind each one, and how to craft an effective answer without sounding like a snake-oil salesman.

Barricades

Avoid sending negative signals during the interview. Crossing your arms sends signals that you are feeling defensive and can suggest that you're hiding something or are defiant. If you cross your legs with an ankle over the opposite knee, this sends the same negative signal.

The Last of the Small Talk

As you and the interviewer get settled in your seats the last of the small talk is being exchanged. Now the real challenge begins as the questions start flying. How to handle those questions—how to turn job interviews into job offers—is the topic of the next two chapters.

CHAPTER 8

MEET YOUR INTERVIEWERS: WHY THEY DO THE THINGS THEY DO

Sitting in front of the interviewer, your mind racing with the possibilities of what could happen next as he looks over your resume, you are probably thinking, "This is crazy. Why am I here? I'd rather be abducted by aliens." What probably won't occur to you is that quite a lot of the time the interviewer feels the same way.

A manager's job is to get work done through others, and the first step is to hire the right people, because if you cannot hire effectively, you can never manage productively, and if you can't manage productively . . . you lose your job. Consequently, most managers learn how to interview effectively. You can also rely on just about all corporate recruiters and HR people to run competent interviews because it's what they do every day.

> You got the interview because the recruiter saw something she liked during the sourcing, screening, and informal background checks via social media. Know that you're one of the few that made the first cut, and walk in with some confidence!
>
> **Mark Babbitt,** CEO and Founder, *www.youtern.com*

How Interviews Are Organized

Experienced interviewers know how the interview is going to progress and the topics they want to address. They know what they are going to ask, why they are asking it, when they are going to ask it, and what they hope to find. They have a plan, and this is what it looks like from the other side of the desk:

How interviews are organized

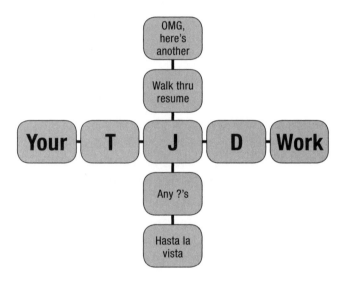

"OMG, Here's Another One"

That's the first thought in the interviewer's mind as you sit down to begin the interview. It continues, "I hope this is the one. All I want is someone who 'gets' the job, can do it and wants to do it, comes to work on a regular basis, and gets on with people. I just need to hire someone and move on to the next project!" Notice that they're not asking for the moon; they're not looking for someone as special as mommy always told you that you were. They just want the basic competencies and attitude *Knock 'em Dead: Secrets & Strategies for First-Time Job Seekers* has taught you to develop.

> If you have two or more candidates who are all similarly qualified, it ultimately comes down to interview preparation, apparent culture fit, motivation, and genuine interest in the opportunity and company.
>
> **Chris Perry,** Brand and Marketing Generator, *www.careerrocketeer.com*

Contrary to what you may think, *the interviewer wants you to relax.* That's because a more relaxed you is a more communicative you, and the interviewer wants lots of information on which to base his decision. So at the beginning of any interview you'll move through some formulaic small talk and the offer of a beverage to prepare the way for the actual questioning to begin. Always accept the beverage, and ask for water. You *are* nervous, so your throat is more prone to dryness, and water is the best remedy.

The interview gets underway with a statement from the interviewer, who will say something along the lines of, "We're looking for a _____ , and I want to find out about your experience and the strengths you can bring to our team." She will then explain a bit about how the interview itself will go: whether you'll be talking to other people, and if so, who they are. This is the time to offer a nicely formatted version of your resume, because next the interviewer is going to glance down at the resume and say, "So tell me a little bit about yourself . . ."

Walk Through Your Resume

> Who gets hired and why? People with confidence and humility are the ones who get hired. You have to be self-confident without being cocky. Recognize what people established in their careers or at the company can teach you.
>
> **Lori Ruff,** CEO, *www.integratedalliances.com*

Interviewers will use your resume as a roadmap of your history and potential capabilities. They will typically walk through your educational and any work history, asking you straightforward questions about different aspects of your experience. A good interviewer wants to limit her contributions to about 20 percent of the interview, leaving you to talk the other 80 percent of the time—offering her plenty of time to analyze your answers. When the conversation turns to work experience and/or your understanding of the target job, your answers should be straightforward, and you should make every effort to show an understanding of your job's deliverables.

Let me explain this word "deliverables"—it's important. Your job has a list of responsibilities, and with each of those responsibilities your manager will expect you to deliver certain results. Combined, the results you deliver determine whether your performance is acceptable or not.

For a salesperson, the job description might talk in general terms about sales, but the deliverable is that you are expected to close x number of sales per week. An accountant's job description might mention the need for Accounts Receivable skills; the deliverable is that the accountant is expected to get all those receivables into the bank account within thirty days.

This brings us to *delivering* on your deliverables: Things don't always go as planned. For example, people (and corporations) don't always have the money to pay their bills on time. Consequently, for the accountant in our example, "deliverables" also embraces the ability to *identify, prevent, and solve problems*—like delinquent accounts; the same applies in your chosen profession.

Deliverables are just the abstract skills you describe in your resume, only translated into the concrete contributions you'll make on a daily basis. Show the interviewer your understanding that in essence the job is about *problem identification, prevention, and solution*. As an entry-level candidate, you aren't expected to have a track record, just an appreciation of the issues and a willingness to learn. This alone will dramatically advance your candidacy. If you've gone the extra mile and talked to people doing the job, you will be able to demonstrate not just a willingness to learn but even a basic working knowledge of the tasks you are likely to face.

Some interviews end after this journey through the resume, either because the interviewer has enough information to rule you out, or because he doesn't know any better. Skilled interviewers use this walk through the resume as a qualifying round. If you pass, they'll take the interview to the next level.

> Employers decide whether or not they want to work with you over the next few years. They hire people they like.
>
> **Sultan Camp,** Military Transition and Social Network Specialist, *www.zeiders.com*

Your TJD Work Pays Off

> **They quickly determine** whether you can "walk and chew gum." Then they drill down into your accomplishments, especially the "how."
>
> **Ron Weisinger,** Principal, DevelopmentLINKS Consulting

An experienced interviewer will want to examine your credentials and any experience you have in each of the job's areas of responsibility. Fortunately, if you have followed the *TJD* process, you will have a clear understanding of the credentials and possibly even experience that you bring to the table. When we worked on your resume, I told you this analysis of the job's requirements would pay off a second time at interviews. Now you're going to start reaping the dividends.

Fresh out of school, you will not be expected to have much experience, so the bar is set much lower than it will be in coming years. However, if you intend to get your career off to a successful start, you will have invested time in contacting your seniors in the profession and asking them about the responsibilities of the job, making sure to connect them to your *transferable skills, professional values,* and the *identification, prevention, and solution of problems.*

Your research allows you to connect any topic the interviewer raises with the qualifications and understanding of the job that you bring to the table. And while you lack experience and often will not be able illustrate your answers with professional-world examples, you might be able to cite a college experience that utilizes the relevant *transferable skills* or *professional values*.

Any Questions?

> You can also ask for feedback: "What could I change about myself and my experience to make me a better fit for the position and the company?"
>
> **Phyllis Mufson**, Career Coach, *www.phyllismufson.com*

You know the interview is drawing to a close when you are asked if you have any questions. Until an offer is on the table, the only questions you want to ask are ones that will give you greater insight into the job or bring that offer closer to the table. This means you need to stay away from questions about the things you are dying to know, such as pay and benefits. There's plenty of time for these questions once an offer is made, but right now asking about salary doesn't get you one inch closer to an offer, so winners stick to the questions that will bring them closer to a job offer.

You need to have the right focus going into the interview. *You are not going to the interview to decide if you want the job*, because you have nothing to decide until an offer is on the table. You are at the interview for one reason only: *to get a job offer*. Nothing else matters. When you consistently focus yourself on getting the offer, you will hone your interview skills; at this point, salary questions are a distraction at best.

Still, you shouldn't be afraid to ask questions, not only at the end, but throughout the interview. Your questions show interest, and we make our judgments of people based on both the statements they make and the questions they ask. The interviewer's answers deliver insights into the job that you wouldn't otherwise have, giving you a better focus for your responses and the points you want to make.

Three great closing questions:

- Are there any reservations you have about my fit for the position that I could try to address?
- This job sounds like something I'd really like to do—is there a fit here?
- Now that we've talked about my qualifications and the job, do you have any concerns about my being successful in this position?

Hannah Morgan, Job Search Strategist, *www.careersherpa.net*

This is especially important when the interviewer does not give you the openings you need to sell yourself. Always have a few intelligent questions prepared to save the situation. See the answer to the question "Do you have any questions?" at the end of Chapter 9.

Hasta la Vista, Baby

At the end of the interview, the interviewer will thank you for your time and may give you some idea of next steps. If this information isn't offered, ask if there is another round of interviews, then:

- Recap your understanding of the job
- Explain that you are qualified and very interested, and reiterate why you are interested
- Ask to schedule the next interview

If there are no more interviews, ask when the decision will be made. Then repeat the above steps, but instead of asking for the next interview ask for the job. You have everything to gain and nothing to lose; showing *motivation* and *intelligent enthusiasm* for the job now could be the decisive factor.

RESOURCES More on interviewers' question strategies in the latest annual edition of *Knock 'em Dead: The Ultimate Job Search Guide.*

CHAPTER 9

KNOCK 'EM DEAD AT THE INTERVIEW

Of all the steps you will take up the ladder of success over the years, none is more difficult than getting a foot on that first rung. You have no idea how the professional game is played, and you are up against thousands of other grads with pretty much the same value proposition to offer.

Interviewers will look at what you have done to show initiative, and how willing you are to learn, grow, and get the job done. Your goal is to stand out from all the other entry-level candidates as someone altogether different: You want to be seen as more knowledgeable than your competition about the job and the world in which it functions, as well as more prepared to listen, learn, and do whatever it takes to earn your place on a professional team. You want to be seen as someone completely engaged in the success of your professional life.

> Go to the interview with an open and curious mind to learn everything you can about the opportunity, the interviewer, the company, the hiring manager, and your coworkers. Asking the right questions will help you come across as much more excited, engaged, and confident.
>
> **Chris Perry**, Brand and Marketing Generator, *www.careerrocketeer.com*

This chapter covers some of the toughest and most frequently asked questions you will face at a job interview. If you take into account wording variations, they cover *just about every* question you will face.

Don't waste time memorizing the following responses; that would be missing the point. This chapter is about understanding the logic behind interview questions. Your answers will come from your research and the *TJD* work you did for your resume.

Knock 'em Dead Answers to Tough Interview Questions

Whenever a question is asked, it is useful to pause for a moment or two to collect your thoughts before answering: that pause shows that you think before you speak, an admired trait in the professional world and a strategy that demonstrates your possession of *critical thinking skills*.

There are no magical answers to an interviewer's questions, but with an understanding of what's behind them, what you have to offer, and an understanding of how and why your targeted professional world works the way it does, you can be prepared with answers that are genuine, honest, *and* advance your candidacy.

Tell me a little about yourself.

> The first question is always the hardest because it is often open-ended. Answer it well without going too long and you'll create some early positive momentum.
>
> **Tim Tyrell-Smith,** Founder, *www.timsstrategy.com*

The interviewer knows that you are nervous and that talking will help you relax. She wants to know about your qualifications for this job, any relevant experience you might have, and whether these considerations warrant your being interviewed. Give a well-considered answer and you set the tone for your candidacy and immediately feel more confident.

You already have the answer to this question prepared:

- Doing your *TJD* exercise helped you determine how employers prioritize the deliverables of this job.
- The *TJD* process also suggested steps to identify your development of *transferable skills* and *professional values*.
- Your social network research gave you insight into the day-to-day demands in each area of responsibility and into the *identification, prevention, and solution of problems* in each area of responsibility.
- The Performance Summary that kicks off your resume captures your qualifications and *motivation* for this job in a few short sentences.

Your answer to this question takes the essence of your Performance Summary and turns it back into full sentences. You won't have a wealth of relevant experience to call on, but you can use the above considerations to your advantage: "I recently graduated with a _____ degree and I've always been interested in _____ . . ."

Here you might give thirty seconds of detail about your life, if it adds to the story, but after that move back to your qualifications: "I worked my way through school in largely menial jobs, but I learned skills that are relevant to this work. The main responsibilities of this job are _____ , _____ , and _____ , and execution of these duties require [*relevant transferable skills*], as well as good *multitasking* and *problem-solving skills*, which I developed in all of my _____ jobs.

"I don't have much real-world experience, but I do understand the challenges that are at the heart of this job. For example, when I was doing a long-term group project in _____ class, we had _____ problem.

"I understand that there are ways I can prevent these problems from arising. For example, _____ .

"And I understand that when things do go wrong, I need to be able to _____.

"The most important thing you need to know about me is that I am not here by accident. I want to make my career in this profession."

Where do you want to be five years from now? What are your future vocational plans?

The mistake all entry-level professionals make is to say, "In management," because they think that shows drive and ambition. But it has become such a trite answer that it immediately generates a string of questions most recent graduates can't answer, questions like, "A manager in what area?" and, "What is a manager's job?" Your safest answer identifies you with the profession you are trying to break into and shows you have your feet on the ground: "I want to get ahead in _____, but without real experience it is difficult to see where the opportunities will be and how my skills will develop to meet them. I intend to quickly develop a clear understanding of how to deal with the problems and challenges that lie within my area of responsibility. I know that I want to make a home in this profession and channel my skills into my profession's areas of growth, and with the support of a good manager, I think these plans will unfold in a logical manner. Right now I need the opportunity to roll up my sleeves and start earning that expertise."

What type of position are you interested in?

Tell the interviewer you are interested in an entry-level job, which is what you will be offered anyway. "I am interested in an entry-level position that will enable me to learn this business from the ground up and will give me the opportunity to grow professionally once I prove myself."

Are you looking for a permanent or temporary job?

The interviewer wants reassurance that you are genuinely interested in the position and won't disappear in a few months. Go beyond saying, "Permanent." Explain why you want the job: "I am looking for a permanent job. I intend to make my career in this field, and I want the opportunity to build a solid foundation in the profession and learn from experienced professionals."

Why do you think this job/industry will sustain your interest over the long haul?

You can expect interviewers to ask questions that gauge your level of interest. You need to know what is going on in whatever profession and industry you intend to enter, because you will be asked.

Your answer should speak both to your pragmatism and your motivation. "I have always been interested in [*your new profession/industry*]. I believe it offers stability and professional growth potential over the years [*explain why*]. Also, I'll be using skills [*itemize strong skill sets that are relevant to the job*] that are areas of strength, from which I derive great personal satisfaction."

What do you know about the company?

Your knowledge of the job and the company is a piece of the jigsaw puzzle that helps the interviewer evaluate your *enthusiasm* and *motivation* for the work

While company research will help you answer the question, your research will also have raised questions; you can use these questions to *turn a one-sided examination of skills into a two-way conversation between professionals with a common interest.* You can wrap up your answer with a question that shows your research: "I read that _____, and wonder how this is affecting you?"

How did you get your summer jobs?

Employers look favorably on recent graduates who have any work experience, no matter what it is. It is far easier to get a fix on someone who has worked while at school: They manage their time better and are more realistic and mature. Any work experience gives you and the interviewer much more in common. So, as you think about some of those crummy jobs you held, take the time to think, in hindsight, about what you actually learned about the professional world from those experiences.

It's not the job that defines you, it's what you bring to the job that defines you; countless successful people in all professions trace their big breaks back to going above and beyond with menial jobs. At any job you can learn that business is about making a profit, that making a profit means taking care of the little things . . . and that when you are starting out, your job is just dealing with the little things. You also learned about doing things more efficiently, *working together as a team*, *solving problems*, adhering to *systems and procedures* (which are always there for good reason), and putting in whatever effort it took to get the job done right. In short, you treated your summer jobs, no matter how humble, as a launch pad for greater things.

In this particular question, the interviewer may also be looking for initiative, *creativity*, and flexibility. Here's an example: "In my town, summer jobs were hard to come by, but I applied to each local restaurant for a position waiting tables, called the manager at each one to arrange an interview, and finally landed a job at one of the most prestigious. I was assigned to the afternoon shift, but because of my quick work, accurate billing, and ability to keep customers happy, they soon moved me to the evening shift. I worked there for three summers, and by the time I left, I was responsible for the training and management of the night-shift waiters, the allotment of tips, and the evening's final closing and accounting. All in all, my experience showed me the mechanics of a small business and of business in general."

What college did you attend, and why did you choose it?

The college you attended isn't as important as your reasons for choosing it—the question examines your reasoning process. Emphasize that it was your choice, and that you didn't go there as a result of your parents' desires or because generations of your family have always attended the Acme School of Welding. Focus on the practical: "I went to _____; it was a choice based on practicality. I wanted a school that would give me a relevant education and prepare me for the real world. _____ has a good record for turning out students fully prepared to take on responsibilities in the real world. My school certainly taught me some big lessons about the value of [*transferable skills* and *professional values*] in the world of business."

How did you pay for college?

Avoid saying, "Oh, Daddy handled that." Your parents may have helped out, but if you can, emphasize that you worked part-time as much as you could. People who pay for their own education make big points with employers because it shows *motivation*, and the experience always delivers a better grasp of the professional world. If this isn't you, find and listen to someone who can tell you what working in the professional world teaches you, and use that knowledge.

Do you think employers should consider grades?

If your grades were good, the answer is obviously "yes." If they weren't, your answer needs a little more thought: "Of course, an employer should take everything into consideration. Along with grades, there should be an evaluation of real *motivation* and *manageability*, the candidate's understanding of how business works, and actual work experience; plus, the best academics don't always make the most productive professionals. Einstein and Edison, two of the most productive minds of modern times, had terrible academic records."

> Listen to the question. The most important information in a sentence is in the second half.
>
> **Marjean Bean, CPC**, President, MedIT Staff

What would your references say?

Even without work experience you may still be asked for references. If you checked your references—and you should—you can give details of what they will say. If you really can't come up with any work references, you should go out and get a part-time job now that will give you some.

For more information on references, read the more extensive discussion in the latest annual edition of *Knock 'em Dead: The Ultimate Job Search Guide.*

What aspects of this job do you consider most crucial?

An interviewer asks this question to examine your grasp of a typical working day. Your answer itemizes the most important responsibilities of the job (you prioritized these in your *TJD*) and then proceeds to address:

1. The *technical skills*: "I need to be able to do [*technical skills*] to execute my responsibilities."
2. Your knowledge of some of the problems that typically occur in each of these areas.
3. Your *transferable skills* and *professional values* as they help you deliver on (1) and (2).

Why do you think you would like this type of work?

Answering requires you to have researched job functions. Earlier I suggested you network with people already doing this job. Ask what the job is like and what that person does day-to-day, what are the challenges related to each major responsibility of the job, and how that person executes his work in ways that *anticipate and prevent these problems* from arising. Armed with these insights into the realities of the job, you can show that you understand what you are getting into. "I think the big challenges with this job are _____ , and helping people solve their problems is just the kind of work I enjoy."

I'd be interested to hear about some things you learned in school that could be used on the job.

The interviewer wants to hear about *real-world* skills, so explain what the experience of college taught you about the world of work, rather than specific courses. Use internships or any work experience to differentiate yourself.

You can find examples in every college activity that gave you the opportunity to develop *transferable skills* and *professional values*. Your answer might say, in part, "Within academic and other on-campus activities, I always looked for the opportunity to apply and develop some of the practical skills demanded in the professional world, such as _____."

What have you done to educate yourself for this job and profession outside of the classroom?

This question examines your initiative/motivation and your understanding of the job's deliverables. Talk about connecting with people who are doing the job, the questions you asked and why you asked them, and what you learned in the process. Even if you do nothing more than walk an interviewer through the research steps you applied from earlier chapters, you will impress her with your analytical skills, plain common sense, and the thorough grasp of the job you gained as a result. Naturally, any internships or related work experience can be cited in your answer.

How do you handle deadlines?

This examines the *time management* and *organizational skills* that enable you to *multitask* productively. You should go through the Plan, Do, Review cycle we addressed in Chapter 2. If you never had a work experience where you employed these skills, you used it when juggling exams, papers, and presentations at the end of each semester.

What is your greatest strength?

This is a wide-open opportunity to talk about *all* your major selling points. Talk first about any relevant *technical skills* you possess. Then talk about your stronger *transferable skills*, and how they are applied in this job. Use these comments as a run-up to your greatest strength, something you know an employer is hoping to find when hiring a recent grad—*intelligent enthusiasm* and an understanding of the work: ". . . but I think my greatest strength is simply that I am really excited about this work. I don't have experience yet, but because

I am so motivated, I am someone who will listen, learn, work hard, ask questions, and give every assignment my best effort. My greatest strength? I think I understand the real guts of the job, and I am motivated to be successful and make a career in this profession."

What is your greatest weakness?

You *are* going to be asked this question, usually right after you have been asked about your greatest strength. Your best option is to talk about a weakness that you share with every other working professional: staying current with the rapid changes in technology that affect every job. Your answer can address how technology has changed the way you learn, the way we communicate, and the way profession-relevant technology has similarly evolved while you were in school.

First talk about these constantly evolving challenges, then follow up with examples that show how you *are* struggling to learn something that is on the very cutting edge. "I'm currently learning [*this new application*] . . ."; "I just attended a webcast on . . ."; "I'm signed up for classes at . . ." With this type of answer you identify your weakness as *something that is only of concern to the most dedicated and forward-looking professionals in your field.*

You could also point to your lack of experience as your greatest weakness; since you will inevitably be competing for an entry-level position, this is a weakness you will share with almost every other first-time job seeker.

How do you approach problems?

There is an established approach to problem solving that every successful professional follows:

- Define the problem.
- Identify why it's a problem and who it's a problem for.
- Identify what's causing the problem.
- Seek input from everyone affected by the problem.
- Identify possible solutions.

- Identify the time, cost, and resources it will take to implement each option.
- Evaluate the consequences of each solution.
- Decide upon the best solution, based on these considerations.
- Identify the steps necessary to solve the problem.
- Build a plan of action that will deliver the solution by any deadline.
- As necessary, gain management approval.
- Execute the steps necessary to solve the problem.

What is your role as a team member?

Companies exist and grow due to their ability to *solve complex problems* for their customers, and complex problems require *teamwork*. Your target job is *a small cog in the complex machinery* that is a successful corporation, and for each cog to function efficiently, it must mesh seamlessly with all the other cogs.

Your department, in turn, has a similar but larger role in that complex money-making machinery. Your ability to link your job's role to that of the department's larger responsibilities will demonstrate your awareness of the importance of *teamwork*.

Have you ever had difficulties getting along with others?

This question examines your people skills and, by extension, your *manageability*. Are you a *team player*, or are you going to be a cog that doesn't mesh, and so disrupts the department's functioning and makes the manager's life miserable?

You can give a yes-or-no answer and shut up, but if you think through what you are going to say, your answer can also emphasize *transferable skills* and *professional values*. You can say that there are two types of people in every department: those who are engaged and committed to peak performance every day, and those who do their work but without the same level of *commitment*. You get on with everyone, but tend to bond more with the people who take a genuine *pride* in becoming their best.

What kinds of decisions are most difficult for you?

You want to position yourself as someone who's decisive but not precipitate, someone who considers causes, options, and their effects on existing *systems and procedures* and company priorities. Note that with unfamiliar situations at work you should always seek input from others.

Think about a real-world example that illustrates your approach. Ideally your example should address some aspect of work you have done, but failing that you can discuss a college project that can be related to the job. Itemize the steps you took in analyzing the problem, and talk about how they helped you reach a logical decision.

What do you like least/find most boring about this job?

The safest approach is to keep your answer focused on those aspects of the job that *everyone* agrees are boring or frustrating, and end your answer on a positive note about how you deal with them: You take the rough with the smooth, and take the time to do _____ well so you don't have to do the damn thing over. It is important that your answer show you remaining objective and calm.

Describe a situation where your work or an idea of yours was criticized.

This is a doubly dangerous question because you are being asked to describe how you handle criticism, as well as to detail inadequacies. If you have the choice, describe a poor idea that was criticized, not poor work. For example, you might choose to describe a situation where a paper you wrote for a class was criticized. If you describe work that was criticized, put your example in the past, make it small, and show what you learned from the experience. You:

- Listen to understand
- Confirm the understanding
- Ask for guidance
- Confirm the desired outcome
- Show a satisfactory resolution
- Address what you learned and how the experience helped you grow

In closing, you recognize the positive impact of the professor, manager, or whoever dispensed the criticism, and how your thinking, approach, and actions have changed as a result. Live by this in your career going forward and you won't go wrong.

Tell me about a time things went wrong.

You are being asked to talk about something that went wrong, but that doesn't mean you can't do so with an example that turned out fine. Your *TJD* process identified a number of such examples you can use. Choose an example and paint it black, but don't point the finger of blame; crap happens.

Your answer needs to identify the event, what caused it, what the effects were, and how you thought through the options and ultimately decided on a course of action that both resolved the problem and found you learning a valuable lesson in the process. You can go on to explain that the next time you faced the same kind of problem you had a better frame of reference.

How have you benefited from your disappointments/mistakes?

You learn more from failures, mistakes, and errors than you do from success, so this is an opportunity for you to demonstrate your *emotional maturity* (you stay calm) and *critical thinking skills* (you think things through objectively).

Your answer will explain how you treat setbacks as learning experiences: you look at what happened, why it happened, and how you can do things differently at each stage. You don't need to be specific about your failures, but be prepared with an example in case of a follow-up question starting, "Tell me about a time when . . . "

Have you ever had any financial difficulties?

If your target job requires working with money or highly confidential information, you are especially likely to face this question. Smile and say, "I just graduated with student loans." If you have experienced financial difficulties, you must tell the truth, because when background checks are made—and they always will be—your credit history is at the top of the checklist.

Have you ever been convicted of a DWI?

You do your best to explain your situation as something that is in your past—something you regret, a one-time unfortunate incident that does not define you and that you hope will not preclude you from securing employment.

Sean Koppelman, President, *www.thetalentmagnet.com*

Find out if it will show up on your record: as this differs from state to state, it will affect how you answer the question. If the application requests this information, and if it will show up, you must answer; otherwise don't offer it until background checks are close. Then be brief and stress what sobering lessons you learned from the experience. Try to get it expunged: Google *DWI expunge.*

Have you ever been convicted of a felony?

First determine if it's on your record; most background checks go back seven years (no more), and states handle criminal records differently, as they do the information an employer may inquire about. Learn what you have to disclose to an employer, and don't disclose more than you have to. Discrepancies between your application and convictions can cause problems. There's no need to discuss issues that didn't result in conviction or anything that has been expunged. Your answer should be brief, with an emphasis on the event being in the past and on what you learned. Never try to minimize the mistake by laying blaming on others.

How do I get the best out of you?

The interviewer could be envisioning you as an employee. Encourage this thought by saying that you are eager to learn and do a good job. Then describe a supportive manager who outlines projects and expected results at the start, notes deadlines, shares her greater experience and perspective, and tells you about potential *problems*: how to *recognize, prevent, and solve* them. You agree on a plan of attack for the work, and how and when you need to give status updates along the way.

What have you done that shows initiative and willingness to work?

You might tell a story about how you landed or created a job for yourself, or got involved in volunteer work. Your answer might show that you both handled unexpected problems calmly and anticipated others. Your *motivation* is demonstrated by the ways you overcome obstacles. For example: "I was working in a warehouse and found that a shipment was due; I knew that room had to be made. I came in on a Saturday, figured out how much room I needed, cleaned up the mess on the loading dock, and made room in the warehouse. When the shipment arrived, the truck just backed in."

After an effort above and beyond the call of duty, a manager might congratulate you; if so, you can conclude your answer with that endorsement: "The manager happened along just when I was finishing the job and said she wished she had more people who took such pride in their work."

What are you looking for in your first job?

You are there to get a job offer, and only want to address your needs when they will be listened to, which is right after an offer is on the table and you know they want you.

Keep your answer general, and focus on getting a good start to your career, learning to do the job well and building a foundation on which to grow professionally, learning from people with more experience who enjoy their work, and working for a company with a solid reputation.

What qualifications do you have that will make you successful in this field?

There is more to answering this question than reeling off your academic qualifications. You will also want to explain that your skills match the job's responsibilities, and talk about the *transferable skills* and *professional values* that will help you do the job well. Include any relevant work experience to support your argument; even a little experience is a better argument than none.

How do you stay current?

We live in an age of technological innovation, in which the nature of every job is changing as quickly as you turn these pages. This means you must look at ongoing professional education as the price of sustained employability. In your answer, talk about the importance of keeping abreast of changes in the profession. You can refer to:

- Courses you are planning to take
- Books you are reading
- Membership in professional associations
- Membership in online groups
- Subscriptions to professional journals

What achievements are you most proud of?

In talking about your achievements, you will have to come up with examples, and it is a good idea to have illustrations that show you achieving success both as an individual and as part of a team. Don't exaggerate your contributions to major projects—share the success and you will be seen as a *team player*. For example, you might say something like, "I am proud of my involvement with _____ [*explain the task and result*]. I made my contribution as part of that team and learned a lot in the process." Use academic or volunteer experience when you don't have relevant work examples.

Tell me about the most difficult project you've tackled.

If you lack real work examples, try to discuss college projects that parallel the work you will do on the new job. Outline the project and its challenges, your *critical thinking* process to isolate causes and possible solutions, the story of your implementation of the solution, and the value it delivered to your employer.

What have you learned from your work experience?

Even if you have had only the most menial of jobs, you still have learned valuable lessons: that little gets achieved without *teamwork*, and that there's invariably sound thinking behind *systems and procedures*. To get to the root of problems it's better to talk less and listen more. Most of all, you've learned that you can either sit on the sidelines watching the hours go by or you can get involved and make a difference with your presence. You do the latter because you're goal-oriented, time goes quicker when you're engaged, and besides, the relationships you build are with better people.

Do you like routine tasks/regular hours?

The interviewer knows from bitter experience that many recent grads hate routine and are hopeless as employees until they come to an acceptance of routine as a part of life. You appreciate that routine is the efficient cycle of procedures that deliver services and products to the company's customer base, you appreciate that the routine and the repetitive have a role in even the most creative of jobs, and you understand that it is only by paying attention to the repetitive details that the work gets done. If regular hours are required, respond, "A company expects to make a profit, so the doors have to be open for business on a regular basis if I am to receive a regular paycheck."

What would you do if a decision needed to be made and no procedure existed?

This is a question about *systems and procedures* and your *manageability*. Show that while you're more than capable of taking initiative, you're not a loose cannon. Explain that the first thing you'd do would be to discuss the situation with your manager or—if time is tight and that isn't possible—with a superior designated by the manager. That's exactly what the hiring manager wants to hear.

How do you rank among your peers?

The question examines your self-esteem. Look at yourself and your peers in different ways until you can come up with a viewpoint that gives you an edge. In some cases it may be possible for you to quantify this—"I graduated twelfth in my class at MIT with a 4.0 GPA." If you can't say something like this, and perhaps came from a background where such a start was never in the cards, you might talk about being the first person in your family to graduate, or working since you were ten. Your goal is to differentiate yourself from your peers, and in this example to show that you are professionally grounded with a life experience that gives you greater professional maturity than many of your peers.

Have you ever found it necessary to make personal sacrifices to get your work done?

Your answer is most effective when you say "yes" and then illustrate with a story of making special efforts that required personal sacrifice of some kind.

Tell me about a time when an emergency caused you to reschedule your workload/projects.

The question examines if you are likely to let personal preferences take precedence over the professional obligations of your job. The story you tell should illustrate your flexibility and willingness to work extra hours when necessary to meet those educational/professional obligations. Demonstrate that your *transferable skills* like *critical thinking* and *multitasking* allowed you to change course and still meet your obligations . . . without compromising your obligations or having a nervous breakdown.

You might add that your *multitasking skills* not only see you through high-pressure situations, but also allow you to stay on top of your regular responsibilities.

How long will it take you to make a contribution? If I hired you today, what would you accomplish first?

Qualify the question by finding out what is important. You can ask what your interviewer will want you to have achieved in your first thirty days, which projects she considers most important, and in which areas she will need the most rapid contributions. These questions will help define the areas where management is first expecting competency and contributions.

Apart from this, your first goals (and therefore achievements) are to understand your responsibilities, the names and responsibilities of your colleagues, and the *systems and procedures* that guarantee things are done in the prescribed manner.

You can finish by noting that your first achievement will be growing into a functioning member of the team.

How do you take direction?

Can you take direction and criticism not only when it is carefully and considerately given, but more importantly when it *isn't*? Can you follow directions and accept constructive criticism, or are you a difficult, high-maintenance, young know-it-all?

If you take offense easily or bristle when your mistakes are pointed out, you won't last long with any employer. Competition is fierce at the entry level, so take this as another chance to set yourself apart: "Yes, I can take instruction—and more important, I can take constructive criticism without feeling hurt. Even with the best intent, I will still make mistakes, and at times someone will have to put me back on the right track. I know that if I'm ever to rise in the company, I must be open to direction."

What is the most difficult situation you have faced? Would you tell me about a time you felt overwhelmed?

You're really being asked: "What do you consider difficult?" and "How did you handle it?" The interviewer will be evaluating your *critical thinking* and *technical skills*.

As long as you graduated with a reasonable GPA, you can speak about the dreaded finals at the end of each semester. You can talk about conflicting priorities, such as having to work and study when there weren't enough hours in the day. Note that your example will show you juggling *responsibilities*: You won't get any points for describing your heart-wrenching decision between showing up for your internship and spending the afternoon doing keg stands. Your answer should include how you evaluated your conflicting priorities and organized your activities to meet all of your obligations and goals.

How do you develop an understanding of new people?

Every new hire is expected to become a viable part of the group, so you need to get an understanding of the group and its individual members. You have found that the best way to become part of a new team is to be open, friendly, helpful, and ask lots of questions. The answers will give you much-needed insights into the ways of the job, department, and company, plus they help you get to know your coworkers and let your coworkers get to know you.

Tell me about a time when you needed to subordinate your personal goals to help someone else.

Show that you are willing to help others and willing to sacrifice personal goals for a greater common good. Explain that you always try to do your work in a way that enables your colleagues to do theirs with a minimum of disruption, and that you always try to help whenever you can. It's your desire, by hard work and goodwill, to be part of something significant: to be part of a team capable of achievements impossible for an individual.

An illustration can come from educational projects, sports teams, or any work experiences that benefited from people working together toward a common goal. It should show what you sacrificed, and end with what you learned and how that knowledge contributed to your growing professionalism.

What do you think determines progress in a good company?

These pages have given you a clear blueprint for professional advancement. Your answer will reference the deliverables of the job as defined in your *TJD* and the *transferable skills* that help you execute every aspect of your job effectively, thereby becoming a productive member of the team.

Finish by referring to the *professional values* of *integrity, commitment,* and a willingness to play by the rules (*systems and procedures*).

> Answers are often too vague, so there are a ton of follow-up questions. Answer the questions more fully and you'll be more satisfied with the flow of the interview.
>
> **Karen McGrath, PHR,** Talent Acquisition Manager, Enterprise Rent-A-Car

How do you handle rejection?

The interviewer wants to know whether you take rejection personally or simply accept it as a temporary rejection of your performance. Here is a sample answer that you can tailor to your particular needs no matter what your job: "I accept rejection as an integral part of the learning process in any pursuit. In fact I think it was Thomas Edison who said that he knew of more ways *not* to invent a light bulb than anyone else on earth . . . I see rejections and problems as learning experiences." You can explain how you consciously work through rejection experiences.

- Define what is being rejected.
- Ask yourself what was the cause of the rejection: an unattainable goal or just the way you went about achieving it?
- Identify what could have been done differently.
- Ask for guidance from your manager and others who have dealt with similar problems.
- Listen and confirm your understanding.
- Identify potential solutions: Reframe the goal and/or the means of achieving it.
- Identify the time, cost, and resources it would take to implement each of your solutions.
- Evaluate the consequences of each approach to parties affected by your actions.
- Decide upon the best solution given these considerations.

- Identify the steps necessary to solve the problem, and build a plan of action that will deliver the solution by any deadline.
- Seek input on your proposed plan of action from your manager and others who have dealt with similar problems. Ask for guidance, listen to the answers, and confirm your understanding.
- Implement your approved solution and show a satisfactory resolution.

Tell me about a situation that frustrated you.

The interviewer wants to know how you channel frustration into productivity. This question is about *emotional maturity*, so show yourself to be someone who isn't managed by *emotions*: You acknowledge the frustration, then put it aside in favor of achieving the results you are paid to achieve. Give an example of a difficult situation in which you remained diplomatic, objective, and found a solution that benefited all concerned.

What interests you least about the jobs you've held?

It is likely that your work experience has contained a certain amount of repetition and drudgery, as all starter jobs do. So beware of saying that you hated a particular job "because it was boring." Regardless of your occupation, there is at least one repetitive, mindless duty that everyone groans about, but which nevertheless goes with the territory. The job you liked least or what you liked least about a job, and how you express it, speaks to your willingness to take the ups and the downs that go with every job. Put your answer in the past; perhaps, "Burger King—hated smelling of french fries . . ." Then show that you learned something, too. "When you get involved, there's always something to learn. I learned that _____." End by moving the conversation forward, "Every job I've held has given me new insights. All of my jobs had their good and bad points, but I've always found that if you want to learn, there's plenty to pick up every day. Each experience was valuable." Notice how this response also shows that you are *organized* and possess *critical thinking* and *multitasking skills.*

You should be prepared with examples of things you have learned from those Burger King jobs, and if examples don't jump to your mind as you read this, refer back to the *transferable skills* and *professional values*.

If the question is, "What interests you least about this job?", it's because interviewers want to gauge your understanding of the work, and when you don't have any real-world experience this also evaluates your motivation in researching the job and the profession.

One way to prepare for this question is to make it part of your social networking research; in fact, it might make a good question to ask in one of your LinkedIn group discussions: "What's the least interesting part of the job, and how do you make yourself pay attention to the boring but necessary details?"

> **How to fail.** Focus on "what's in it for me?" Put management in a position where every simple job-related task or request becomes a negotiation. Be intolerant of the short-term sacrifices that lead to the greatest long-term rewards.
>
> **Rick Kean, CPC,** Consultant Emeritus, A. M. Hamilton, Inc.

Tell me a story.

The question is common, so prepare a story that relates to the job in some way and weave in one or more of the *transferable skills* or *professional values* as a subtext: why you chose this degree and this profession, a valuable lesson you learned in an internship or summer job, what you learned about the professional world from researching this job and learning about career management, or perhaps how you came to be sitting at the interview today.

I'm not sure you're suitable for the job.

If you can see a potential problem with an opportunity, the employer probably can too. Nevertheless, you were close enough to get the interview, so make every effort to land the offer. Stay calm. Before you answer, you need to gather more information, so ask, "Why do you say that?"

You might lack experience, as do the other candidates, but with your research into the job's deliverables and your understanding of how *transferable skills* and *professional values* support successful execution of the work, you have the outline for a strong answer. Perhaps finish with, "I may lack experience, but I have a grasp of the job's deliverables equal to candidates far my superior in chronological experience. I want this job, and my motivation and room for growth will make me a better and more reliable employee for a longer time."

Do you have any questions?

A sign that the interview is drawing to a close. Most candidates ask questions about money and benefits, but because *your goal at every interview is to bring the interviewer to the point of offering you the job*, such questions are irrelevant: They don't bring you any closer to the job offer. Concentrate, instead, on questions that will bring your candidacy closer to an offer:

- Who succeeds in this job and why?
- Who fails in this job and why?
- What are the major projects of the first six months?
- What will you want me to have achieved after thirty days?
- What will you want me to have achieved after ninety days?
- What will my first assignments be?

See Chapter 11 for a longer list of the questions you might want to ask. The answers to these questions give you greater insight into the job, will help you make more points about your suitability, and will give you ammunition to make a more powerful closing statement.

At this point in the interview, you should ask about next steps. Are there more interviews? If there are, match your skills to the needs of the job, explain your interest in the job and desire to pursue it, then ask for the next interview.

If there's not another interview, cite your understanding of the job, talk about how your skills match each of the deliverables, say that you want the job and want to join the team, then ask for the job.

What can you do for us that someone else cannot do? Why should I hire you? Why are you the best candidate for the job?

In your *TJD* exercise you prioritized employers' needs and then encapsulated your related skills in the performance summary section of your resume. Review that summary before every interview, because it will help keep you focused on the employer's needs and the points you need to make in response to his questions.

- Demonstrate your grasp of the job's responsibilities and the skills/education you bring to the table.
- Make plain your understanding of the problems that regularly crop up in each area of responsibility. Say that while you don't yet have much practical experience in *problem identification, prevention, and solution*, unlike most of your contemporaries you are aware of and eager to take on new challenges.
- List the *transferable skills* that you developed in school and in any work, internship, or volunteer experience you might have. Say you believe these are the skills that underlie professional competence in the target job.

How much money do you want?

Ask for too much and you might not get an offer; ask for too little and you could be kicking yourself for years. The answer is to *come up with a salary range that puts you in the running, but doesn't nail you down to one specific dollar figure* that you might regret.

> Check *www.salary.com* and *www.payscale.com* to see what you can command given your skills, experience, and geographic location. Next, call the target company's HR department to determine the salary range of the available position.
>
> **Alexandra Levit**, Author, *Blind Spots, www.alexandralevit.com*

All jobs have salary ranges attached to them. Your approach is to come up with a salary range for yourself. With your research you can come up with three different figures:

1. First, given your skills, experience, and location (for example, jobs in Manhattan pay more than most because of cost of living concerns) determine the least you would accept for a suitable job with a stable company.
2. Second, given the same considerations, what would constitute a fair offer for a suitable job with a stable company?

It's important for entry-level candidates to know what the salary range is like in their industry for those just starting out. The worst way to screw up a negotiation is to ask for way more than anyone else is making.

Josh Tolan, CEO, *www.sparkhire.com*

3. Third, given the same considerations, come up with the figure that would make you smile, but which is still within reason.

This gives you three figures: a minimum, a midpoint, and highpoint. Kick out the lowest: You can always negotiate downward. This leaves you with a salary range that you can give with confidence.

Preparation for handling interview questions like these takes time, so don't leave it till the last minute. You are taking a new product to market; accordingly, you've got to analyze what it can do, who is likely to be interested, and how you are going to sell it to them. Start now and hone your skills to get a head start on your peers; you'll get more interviews, and the more you interview, the better you'll get.

RESOURCES For further discussion of tactics for turning interviews into job offers, see the entire second half of *Knock 'em Dead: The Ultimate Job Search Guide*, latest annual edition.

PART IV
AFTER THE INTERVIEW

CHAPTER 10

OUT OF SIGHT CAN MEAN
OUT OF MIND

Studies have shown that the last person interviewed more frequently gets the job, but this isn't always the case. Even if you are the last one interviewed, the longer the decision-making period, the less distinct candidates become from each other in the hiring manager's memory. You leave your interviewers with a strong, positive image, and you don't want that memory to slip with the passage of time and a busy schedule. A good follow-up strategy could well be the deciding factor in who gets the job offer if the race is tight between you and another candidate.

> Most job seekers do not follow up after an interview. Follow up and this could be a deciding factor.
>
> **Jessica Hernandez,** President, *www.greatresumesfast.com*

As soon as you can after the interview, make notes on what happened. The information will help with your follow-up with this company, and reviewing all your follow-up notes after two or three interviews may alert you to a weakness you hadn't noticed. *Self-awareness, that rare ability to look at oneself objectively, is always the first step in fixing behavioral and performance problems.* Make notes on these categories:

- Who did you meet? What were their titles and e-mail addresses?
- What did you find out about the job?
- What are its first projects/challenges?

- Why can you do it? What are the problems?
- What went right and why?
- What went wrong and why?
- What was a royal screw-up and why?
- What did the interviewer say on any topic related to the job, company, competition, industry, or profession that might give you a unique follow-up, were you to Google something interesting?
- What did the interviewer say was the next step?
- Are there other candidates in contention?
- When will a decision be made?
- What did the interviewer say in concluding the interview?

Using the information gathered from this exercise, you can begin a follow-up campaign. Knowing if there is another round of interviews or if the decision is going to be made tomorrow afternoon or next week has a significant impact on how and when you will follow up.

> Those that send follow-up notes show the employer how they feel about the position. Those who don't follow up just don't seem as serious.
>
> **Josh Tolan,** CEO, *www.sparkhire.com*

The majority of my colleagues suggest you follow up within twenty-four hours, and I agree *if this is the final interview and the decision is imminent*, i.e., within the next seventy-two hours. I think a differently paced schedule is called for when there are more interviews in the cycle and the decision is further away; in these circumstances the follow-up letter's job is to re-energize and maintain the visibility of your candidacy when memory of it is beginning to slip with the passage of time and is blurred by other candidates.

Follow-Up Steps and Pacing

Knowing where you are in the selection cycle will help you execute a well-paced follow-up campaign. We'll start with follow-up after the first interview in a series.

After the First Interview in a Series

Informal First Follow-Up Within Twenty-Four Hours

> Avoid victim statements ("I just need a chance" or "I don't know why I haven't heard from you") and insecure phrases ("I know I'm not the perfect candidate" or "I know you have lots of others to choose from") at all costs!
>
> **Mark Babbitt**, CEO and Founder, *www.youtern.com*

If you can find something interesting related to the job, company, competition, industry, or profession, your first follow-up will be professional-casual, reinforcing the tone of *an ongoing conversation between two professionals with a common interest.* Although you might have been encouraged to use first names during the interview, because you are younger you should revert to the formalities of Mr./Ms. in written communication (probably until an offer is on the table). This will be received as respectful and also demonstrate that you understand professional protocols. If use of first names hasn't been encouraged, don't presume: It won't win you points, while showing professional courtesies always does.

Note the short, punchy, casual yet still professional tone of this sample follow-up e-mail:

"It was great to meet you this afternoon. I really enjoyed talking about the _____ position. Your comments/our conversation on [*the topic of your attachment, or what you paste into the body copy*] has been buzzing in the back of my mind all day. I just ran across this and thought you'd enjoy it."

Send the e-mail between 7:00 p.m. and 10:00 p.m. that evening or early the next morning when you first get up, whichever is closer to the limits of the twenty-four hour mark. Do not send an e-mail during business hours.

Your first meeting will have tagged you as someone different. This initial follow-up aims to continue the differentiation. The tone is respectful, demonstrating your *intelligent enthusiasm* (you are actively engaged in thinking about this job and profession).

Formal First Follow-Up

Your formal first follow-up should arrive two to no later than three days after the first interview, *or* after your first *informal* follow-up—adjusting your timing to the needs of each separate selection cycle. This formal follow-up letter should make the following points:

- The date and time you met with the interviewer and the title of the target job
- You paid attention to what was said in the interview
- Why you can do the job
- You are excited about the job and want it
- You have the skills and professional attitude to contribute to those first major projects as discussed in the interview

Adding New Information

Your follow-up note is also a good opportunity to add new information that you realize would be relevant, to answer any questions you didn't adequately address, or to introduce any aspects of your candidacy that you forgot in the heat of the moment. You can say something along the lines of, "On reflection, I . . ." or "Having thought about our meeting, I thought I'd mention . . ." or "I should have mentioned that . . ."

Keep the note short (less than one page) and address it to the hiring manager or main interviewer if you haven't met your new boss yet. If you interviewed with other people and the meeting was more than cursory, you can send separate e-mails to each.

Additional Interviews

If the selection cycle is normal, three interviews for each of a handful of short-list candidates can take three or four weeks, so with the second and subsequent interviews (excepting the final interview), your follow-up pattern should replicate that of the initial interview.

1. An informal follow-up within twenty-four hours, essentially saying:

    "Good to see you again Ms. _____ and to meet the guys. It was a great opportunity to see the team. Thanks for your time."

    You might replace this with an equally brief phone call, when there is something to warrant a brief conversation. If the manager doesn't pick up, leave a complete but brief message. You don't need to call back.

2. A formal follow-up, following the same principles and timing as before. As the interview cycle progresses, you want to maintain awareness of your candidacy, but you don't want to be seen as doing anything by rote.

Although the bulk of business correspondence these days is done via e-mail, remember that a traditional letter can make you stand out, especially since your competition has never heard of traditional mail.

> While sending an e-mail to thank someone is acceptable, it doesn't set you apart. Sending a thank-you note by traditional mail *does* separate you from the crowd.
>
> **Dr. Larry Chiagouris,** Mentor, *www.thesecrettogettingajobaftercollege.com*

Extended Interview Cycles

You don't want to make a pest of yourself by calling or e-mailing every day, but neither do you want to drop out of sight. If the selection cycle stretches out into a month or more, as it sometimes can, make contact every couple of weeks, but keep it very low-key. You don't want to seem overly anxious, just interested. As you did before, you might send profession-relevant information:

"Mr. _____, being so busy, you may not have seen the article I've attached. It's about new legislation that's bound to affect most companies in the industry.

Regards,

Martin

P.S. I'm still determined to be your next _____."

You can do this in an e-mail and/or by traditional mail.

Getting a funny e-mail always brightens your day, and giving the interviewer a smile is a great way to be remembered, but this requires judgment, something most of your peers and perhaps even you have not yet acquired (many of them never will). Do not send anything of a sexual, political, racial, or religious nature, as it constitutes a breach of *professional values*.

The same considerations apply when sending a cartoon via traditional mail. This works because it's a different delivery medium and the cartoon causes a smile; plus, if you're lucky, the cartoon gets stuck on the wall or passed on.

> If you talked about anything personal in the interview, mention that: "Glad to meet another Thai food lover. Here's the link to the restaurant I mentioned." Now you're even more memorable.
>
> **Leslie Ayres,** Job Search Guru, *www.thejobsearchguru.com*

Reposted Jobs

Sometimes jobs remain open for a long time, or they may be frozen because of budgetary constraints and reposted under a different job title. In these instances, go through an abbreviated *TJD* exercise with the new job title to make sure the job hasn't changed in any meaningful ways and that you have all the relevant keywords. If you're still in touch with the hiring manager or recruiter, send her the customized and updated version of your resume, noting the changes in the company's needs, and subsequently make a follow-up call.

The longer the hiring process drags on, the less likely it is that you will get the offer. It can happen, but the odds get longer as time goes by. Don't let your job search stand still while you're waiting for a response from one company. Remember: *You don't have the job until you have a written offer in hand.*

When the Hiring Decision Is Imminent

A decision next Friday means that an offer will be extended on that date, while the actual decision will be made *at least* seventy-two hours to five days prior—allowing HR the time to shepherd the paperwork through the authorization process. Of course, this isn't the case if you are interviewing for a job today and they tell you the decision will be made at the end of the week. As always, you adapt your follow-up strategy to reflect the demands of the hiring cycle.

If you know in advance that a decision is coming, say Friday of the following week, you can aim to get an e-mail on the hiring manager's desk this Friday/Monday. A slight variation of that message might arrive via traditional mail on the same or following day, and you can make a telephone call no later than Wednesday morning. This leaves seventy-two hours before decision time.

Final Written Communications

The content of these communications should cover:

- "We last met on _____ and have been talking about _____ job."
- "I can do the job and this is why: [talk about the *technical skills* you bring]."

- "I am excited about the job and this is why: [talk about how you can contribute to first projects and your desire to join a great group of people]."
- "I will make a good hire and this is why: [talk about the *transferable skills* and *professional values* you bring to the job]."
- "I want the job. What do I have to do to get it?"

Making That Final Call

If a hiring decision is imminent, succinctly following up on your e-mails and letters within seventy-two hours of decision time might help seal the deal. Work out what you want to say, write it down in bullet points, and make practice calls to a friend, keeping it brief and to the point. Then, when you are ready make the call, you have nothing to lose and a job offer to gain.

RESOURCES Job search letters and templates are available at *www.knockemdead* *.com,* including follow-up, negotiation, acceptance, rejection, resignation, and thank-you letter templates.

CHAPTER 11

JOB OFFER NEGOTIATIONS

A job offer will eventually be put on the table, probably after one or two approach questions about money. These questions may be asked at one of your interviews, or perhaps even over the phone. This is the first time you really have decisions to make: Do you want this job, and on what terms? The issues for your consideration are the job and its potential, the company and its stability, the money and the benefits. Entering into employment negotiation is serious business, and it helps to have the right mindset for the situation. There are two big considerations.

> Most companies should have a pay scale where they assign you a fair wage based on the job and your qualifications. You're not really in a position to negotiate if you don't have a strong track record and you're looking for someone to give you a chance.
>
> **Scott Keenan,** HR Generalist, *www.educatedandinexperienced.blogspot.com*

1. They want you, but if you are like most new entrants into the professional workplace, you have very little bargaining power. You almost entirely lack experience, and you are being offered the job based entirely on an evaluation of your potential.
2. This job has an approved salary range that cannot and will not be tampered with for your benefit. If you are hired, you will be hired within that salary range. If you negotiate too hard, you run the risk of the company moving on to one of the other

acceptable candidates. And because this is an entry-level position, there are always plenty of other acceptable candidates.

You need to understand that you are going to get an offer pretty much like everyone else's, and whether you get a little bit more or a little bit less just *doesn't matter*. What is important is that you are getting a job, you are crossing that final bridge into adulthood, and you are getting a foothold on the bottom rung on the professional ladder of success.

This is just your first job and your career is not going to be a sprint to the top; no matter what you are told, it is a marathon that will be run over many job changes and upwards of fifty years. Put in a proper perspective, the starting salary for this job is the least of your concerns; what's much more important is the experience you will gain and the opportunities it will present. Sooner than you can imagine, two, three, four years are going to whiz by and you will be making your first strategic career move. Then, all of a sudden, money becomes a much more negotiable issue.

Step #1
Open with, "If I understand the job correctly . . ." and then restate the responsibilities of the job and what you bring to the table in each area of responsibility, building into your explanation what you know about the role of the job within the department, any initial or special projects, and any special needs that have come to light in your conversations. Your goal is to demonstrate your thorough grasp of the job. You want the interviewer muttering, "Wow, she really gets it!" Your dialogue sounds something like this: "If I'm qualified for this job, which I am because of A, B, C, D, I feel sure you'll make me a fair offer. What is the salary range for this position?"

Do your research. Know how much the company should be paying you and what your benefits package should look like; *www.glassdoor.com* can help with this.

Leslie Zaikis, Director of Business Development, *www.levoleague.com*

You may then be given a range, and if any part of that range intersects with *your* range (for more on determining your personal salary range see the salary question in Chapter 9), you reply, "Excellent! We certainly have something to talk about, because I was looking for between $45,000 and $55,000. Obviously I'd like $55,000. How close do you think we can get?" or "That's certainly something we can talk about. I'm looking for between $45,000 and a maximum of $55,000. How much flexibility is there?"

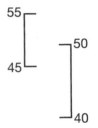

Step #2

If the interviewer declines your request and asks again how much you want, reply with your predetermined salary range, which maximizes the chances of finding a match with the employer's financial parameters and minimizes the odds of you asking for too much or too little. After this, back off the salary question and address benefits and other questions.

Questions to Evaluate the Job

Money is important, but your career trajectory is more so. Your first job is a pivotal point in your life that affects not just this job and the next couple of years, but your whole life going forward. Especially with your first job, you shouldn't ever make a decision based purely on salary without careful consideration of other factors.

This job isn't your goal in life, it's the first step along your chosen path, and you would be wise to determine how this opportunity will serve you as a launching pad, helping you build skills and move toward your goals. To find out, ask questions relevant to your situation. In no particular order, many of the following questions will be things you want to ask.

The Job and Its Potential

- How long has the job been open?
- Why is it open? Who held the job last?
- What is she doing now? Promoted, fired, or quit?
- How long was she in that job?
- How many people have held this job in the last three years? Where are they now?
- How often have people been promoted from this position—and how many, and where to?
- Who in the company was in this position the shortest length of time? Why? Who has remained in this position the longest? Why?

Other questions that might follow include:

- What does it take to succeed in this job?
- Who fails in this job and why?
- What personality traits do you consider critical to success in this job?
- What kind of training does the company provide/encourage/support?
- Why did you choose to work here?
- Tell me about your management style.
- How often will we meet?
- How frequent are performance and salary reviews? Weighted toward merit and performance? If so, how?
- How does the performance appraisal and reward system work? Exactly how are outstanding employees recognized, judged, and rewarded?
- To what extent are the functions of the department recognized as important and worthy of review by upper management?
- Where and how does my department fit into the food chain?
- What does the department hope to achieve in the next two to three years? How will that help the company?

- What do you see as the strengths of the department? What do you see as weaknesses?
- What role do you hope I will play in the department?
- What informal and formal benchmarks will you use to measure my effectiveness and contributions?
- Based on my effectiveness, how long would you anticipate me holding this position? When my position and responsibilities change, what are the possible titles and responsibilities I might grow into?
- What is the official corporate policy on internal promotion? How many people in this department have been promoted from their original positions since joining the company?
- How do I pursue promotion and how do you determine my suitability?
- What training and professional development programs are available?
- How does the company support independent skill development initiatives?
- Does the company sponsor all or part of any costs?
- What are the potential career paths within the company for someone with my job title?
- To what jobs have people with my title risen in the company?

Corporate Culture

All companies have their own way of doing things—that's corporate culture. Not every corporate culture is for you.

> What you can sometimes negotiate is when you will get a salary review with a potential raise. Most companies do this annually, but you can ask for a six-month salary review.
>
> **Dr. Kate Duttro,** Career Coach for Academics, *www.careerchangeforacademics.com*

- What do you see as the company's mission? What are the company's goals?
- What approach does this company take to its marketplace?
- What is unique about the way this company operates?
- What is the best thing you know about this company? What is the worst thing you know about this company?
- How does the reporting structure work? What are the accepted channels of communication and how do they work?
- What kinds of checks and balances, reports, or other work-measurement tools are used in the department and company?
- What advice would you give me about fitting into the corporate culture? About understanding the way you do things here?
- Will I be encouraged or discouraged from learning about the company beyond my own department?

Company Growth and Direction

For those concerned about employment stability and career growth, a healthy company is mandatory.

- What expansion is planned for this department, division, or facility?
- What is your value proposition to prospective customers?
- When you lose a deal, to whom do you lose it?
- What markets does the company anticipate developing?
- Does the company have plans for mergers or acquisitions?
- Currently, what new endeavors is the company actively pursuing?
- How do market trends affect company growth and progress? What is being done about them?
- What production and employee layoffs and cutbacks have you experienced in the last three years?
- What production and employee layoffs and cutbacks do you anticipate? How are they likely to affect this department, division, or facility?

- When was the last corporate reorganization? How did it affect this department? When will the next corporate reorganization occur? How will it affect this department?
- Is this department a profit center? How does that affect remuneration?

Negotiating Benefits

Once a base salary is on the table and you've given it one shot at a bump upward, ask questions that give you more information with which to evaluate the opportunity. Then address benefits and other incentives. These can be an important compensation if the initial offer is lower than you wanted. For instance, you can ask about:

- A signing bonus
- A performance review after a specified number of days (90/120), followed by a raise
- A title promotion after a specified period
- A year-end bonus
- Stock options
- 401(k) and other investment-matching programs
- Compensation days for unpaid overtime/travel
- Life insurance
- Financial planning and assistance
- Paid sick leave
- Personal days off
- Profit sharing
- Vacation

You can ask these questions over the phone, or request another meeting to review these points. I prefer the latter, because you get to meet everyone as the new member of the team and the boss is buoyant because she can at last get back to work. Plus there is the *slight* concern that you might jump ship and leave them back at square one. These factors encourage agreement with reasonable requests.

> Find one key thing that matters to you and explain *why* it matters to you, and you have a much better chance of a successful negotiation.
>
> **Tim Tyrell-Smith,** Founder, *www.timsstrategy.com*

You may get nothing more than the standard package, but you have nothing to lose by asking and everything to gain. Once the package is straightened out, you can come back to the base salary one last time, but remember always to negotiate in a friendly and cooperative way. The response to this will be your final offer.

Employment Obligations and Restrictions

> Items not in the "salary" budget are often easier to negotiate. Perhaps you can negotiate an annual trip to a conference or professional training that will enhance your skills, making you more valuable.
>
> **Kathryn Minshew,** Founder and CEO, *www.thedailymuse.com*

- Any verbal offer you accept is dependent on the offer being in writing and you being comfortable with what's in the employment agreement. Translation? As you will come to learn over the years, verbal offers cannot be trusted or relied upon at all. Pay careful attention to what the company will ask of you in signing the agreement. Employment contracts are legal documents designed to obfuscate and intimidate the neophyte. You can and should take the time to have them explained to you, and then take them home and see if you agree with the interpretation given. If in doubt, take it to career services, and if the numbers are significant enough to warrant the expense, have an employment lawyer review it. The following are some contractual issues you may wish to think about:

- Assignment of Inventions
- Non-Disclosure Clauses
- Non-Compete Clauses
- Severance and Outplacement
- Relocation

For a more extensive discussion of these topics, go to the *Secrets & Strategies for First-Time Job Seekers* page at *www.knockemdead.com.*

Accepting the Offer

The process of negotiating the offer may take some time, but when it's concluded be sure to mention how excited you are about the new job. Reply to the offer in a formal written letter. If you have held a stop-gap job while pursuing your first step, never resign your current position until you have an offer in writing, because offers can and do get withdrawn for a thousand reasons beyond your control.

RESOURCES There is extensive advice about follow-up and negotiating an offer in the latest annual edition of *Knock 'em Dead: The Ultimate Job Search Guide.*

Templates for follow-up, negotiation, acceptance, rejection, resignation, and other job-search letters are available at *www.knockemdead.com.*

PART V
LIFETIME CAREER-MANAGEMENT STRATEGY: HOW TO GET WHAT YOU WANT OUT OF LIFE

CHAPTER 12

STARTING ON THE RIGHT FOOT

All too often people join a company and, in an effort to make a powerful impression, achieve just the opposite. How you behave when you first start work will determine your acceptance by management and by the team, your tenure, and your ultimate success with the company.

Here are six rules that will help you avoid cranial-rectal inversion in your first months at your first job, and get this first step of your career started on the right foot.

Rule #1: Make a Positive First Impression

> There will be assignments that don't seem significant, but you'll find the experience much more valuable than the task. Volunteer for anything that broadens your exposure within the company.
>
> **Carl Nielson,** Principal, *www.careercoachingforstudents.net*

Never assume anything when you start your first job, and don't try to change the world before you know the way to the restroom. Your first task is to master your job's responsibilities and get to know the people you work with, as well as the people whose work is affected by yours. One of the smartest minds on the topic of achieving professional success, Rick Kean, is dead-on when he suggests, "Nail proficiency in your job first, help pick up slack on necessary but unpopular tasks, and do enough homework to ask intelligent questions."

Remember people's names, and go out of your way to smile and introduce yourself to everyone. Don't overlook clerical staff—it isn't courteous, and allies here can always repay your cordiality down the line. In short, learn the job, the organization, and the people. Work extra hours as necessary without complaint, and form good relationships inside and outside your department.

> If you act like you don't need help from anyone, especially if you're brand new, this is going to make the team less likely to want to work with you.
>
> **Josh Tolan**, CEO, *www.sparkhire.com*

Ask for advice and listen closely to feedback on your performance—you are new at this and pretty much everyone wants you to succeed. Say thank you to everyone who assists you, and show further appreciation of their time and input with brief follow-up notes.

As you get acclimatized over the first few days, you will begin to see the flow of work. Whatever the apparent madness you see in the early days at your first company, there is usually some very sound method behind it. The paychecks don't bounce, so the company's employees and officers must be doing something right. With this in mind, don't make comments about how things should be done, because no one will listen and some will take offense that "the newbie is a know-it-all." That just encourages some wise-ass to put you in your place. Don't be the guy who makes everyone feel like you were hired because they weren't doing anything right and you're there to fix it.

You need time to get to know the company, its services, and its people. In turn, those people need time to get to know you. If you arrive and immediately begin reinventing the company, it will be seen as arrogance and is going to be taken as a personal insult, not an opportunity to bow before a new and awesome deity! No one wants to hear your ideas until they know if you are a talker or a doer.

Rule #2: Meetings Are Minefields

Meetings are minefields for the unwary. You'll be introduced and encouraged to speak up, but don't say too much. Stick to: you're new, happy to be here, have to learn the ropes, and hope you can ask for help and advice as you learn your way around. My colleague Nancy Anton, a senior talent scout at Cigna, advises, "Take notes; make others feel what they say is important enough to write down."

Whatever you do, don't make suggestions until you have been accepted as a member of the team: No one will listen until they know you're worth listening to, and that acceptance will take months. If the idea is really good, and no one has thought of it before you arrived (highly unlikely), another few weeks isn't going to make any difference.

> **How to fail.** Talk more than listen, align yourself with gossips, change procedures, have a negative attitude, miss deadlines, be uncommunicative, don't pitch in to solve problems, and step on others to reach your own goals.
>
> **Jacqui Barrett-Poindexter, MRW, CEIP,** Partner and Chief Career Writer, *www.careertrend.net*

Rule #3: Notice Housekeeping and Dress

In some companies a messy desk signifies an industrious, brilliant creative genius at work. In others it signifies a messy slob who's an embarrassment to the profession. Evaluate everyone's appearance and personal work environment, then emulate the best people one and two ranks above you. When new coworkers are getting to know you, the right dress code and a work environment that reflects the company's best subtly positions you as someone to watch.

Rule #4: Gain Acceptance

During your first ninety days, as you are learning the ropes, management and your coworkers are looking carefully at how you perform and informally accrediting you a status within the group. They evaluate how you are doing your job and whether you execute your duties professionally and with respect for the work and responsibilities of others. They will judge how you treat other people and they will talk about you, so never discuss one employee with another, even if encouraged to do so—it could come back to haunt you.

Your coworkers will notice whether or not you recognize their help and give credit where it's due, whether you shoulder your share of the responsibility for maintaining a friendly, positive workplace, and whether you respect the existing hierarchy within the team.

Rule #5: Communicate with Management

Failure to communicate is the major reason why things "don't work out," and young grads find themselves back on the street. Some companies have extensive *onboarding* programs to help new employees get up to speed; others have little or no such support. At the end of the first day, if you haven't been offered adequate guidance to get started, initiate your own onboarding program.

> Regularly sit down with your manager and talk about how you are doing. Hearing the bad and the good allows you to adjust your sails and set the right course as you navigate your career.
>
> **Hannah Morgan,** Job Search Strategist, *www.careersherpa.net*

Meet with your manager and ask for help "making a good start." Determine your responsibilities and get clear direction on the job's deliverables, what your boss expects you to have achieved by the end of your first month, and how performance is measured. Ask why people fail in this job and how they succeed. Then follow up once a week to report on your progress, receive feedback, and ask for guidance on the coming week. This won't be seen as insecurity or brownnosing if you're straightforward and sincere about trying to learn the ropes and improve as an employee.

The Key to the Inner Circle

After the ninety-day probationary period, keep these informal meetings in your monthly schedule. Management will see you doing things the right way and you will attract the notice of others who are doing well, the members of the inner circle—and that's where special assignments, raises, and promotions live.

Rule #6: Start Small

Take the time to get your feet on the ground, learn your way around, make friends, and absorb the culture. As you do this you'll see plenty of opportunities to make a difference with your presence. Prioritize them and start small, with each project meticulously conceived, planned, and implemented. Under no circumstances discuss any employee with another.

> Listen well, adapt to the culture, and work your tail off to prove your worth.
>
> **Caroline Dowd-Higgins,** Career Director, Maurer School of Law; CBS Radio Host, www.carolinedowdhiggins.com

If you have ideas, the time to start introducing them is sometime after the ninety-day probationary period, when you know:

- The names of everyone in the department
- How the department works and why it works that way
- How the company works and why it works that way
- Who's trustworthy and who isn't

- Management and other power players holding titles at least one and ideally two levels above yours

Start with smaller ideas—they are easier to sell, help you build a foundation of credibility, and should something go wrong, the failure is no big deal. Every department and company has an approved way of "doing things," and you should have a clear understanding of how the *systems and procedures* work before beginning any initiative or project. At the same time, you should understand the hidden hierarchies of power and personality that exist in most departments and companies. The people in these hierarchies are the people who hold the fate of your initiative in their hands. When you start small, you are effectively floating trial balloons whose trajectory will tell you where the power lies and how to get things done without antagonizing the wrong people.

> Learn to capitalize on your skills and assert your achievements. If you don't do it, no one else will, and you'll be out-promoted by people who know how to leverage their contributions. Remember the fine line between confidence and arrogance.
>
> **Alexandra Levit,** Author, *Blind Spots, www.alexandralevit.com*

Additionally, it doesn't hurt for your ideas, when you do introduce them, to be seen as part of a team effort. They will usually carry more initial weight when a member of that inner circle also has ownership. You don't lose credibility sharing the glory with someone of stature; you gain it.

> Pitch in and do whatever needs to get done, even if it's something you'd prefer not to do or feel is beneath you.
>
> **Allison Cheston,** Career Connector, *www.allisoncheston.com*

You don't climb alone; no one does. You will do it most effectively with the support, encouragement, and camaraderie of similarly committed professionals, and as such we grow together. That's why the people at the top of every profession all know each other and have done so for years.

No one likes to be overwhelmed with genius, and the better you are, the more you have to work at your humility. Taking it slowly in the first ninety days will speed your acceptance by the group as a whole and allow you the time to recognize the real players amongst your peers. When it comes to establishing your credibility and visibility, the good news travels more slowly than the bad, but it does travel.

CHAPTER 13

CLIMBING THE LADDER OF SUCCESS

Professional change is a constant in your life. If you want to make your dreams come true, you have to do things differently, and not just in your job search, but also in the way you manage your career. Your first job is a golden opportunity to invent a *professional persona* for yourself and confirm a positive trajectory for your professional life.

> Define positive attitude, take pride in your work, help others whenever you can.
>
> **Joshua Waldman,** Author, *Job Searching with Social Media for Dummies,* *www.careerenlightenment.com*

The Leap of Faith

Believe in yourself, and back up that belief with action. Make this first job the springboard to a successful career. Do everything you can to make this job a success and this company one that you can call home and grow with for many years, but never lose focus on what is best for MeInc's long-term economic survival and prosperity and your personal fulfillment.

Protect Your Job and Boost Your Employability

Of all the skills you need to survive and prosper, *some of the very weakest are the skills of career management, but if MeInc is to survive and prosper these same career management skills are the ones that need to become strengths.* The moment you have settled into your first job and been accepted as a member of the team is the moment most people begin to coast; but coasting doesn't make the day go faster, and it doesn't help you get what you want out of life.

Build Your Core Competencies

Once you get that first job, nurture it, both for the security it brings and as a foundation for future growth. Every day, technology changes the skills you need to compete in the workplace, so if you are not consistently developing new skills, you are being paid for abilities that are rapidly becoming obsolete. Hone the *technical skills* of your job to perfection, until you are not only supremely competent but also better than you ever thought you could be.

> *Work on your weaknesses.* Your strengths get you hired but in order to advance you need to shore up the personal, technical, and transferable skills that keep you from doing a less-than-stellar job.
>
> **Jacqui Barrett-Poindexter, MRW, CEIP,** Partner and Chief Career Writer, *www.careertrend.net*

In the last chapter we established a pattern of regular informal communication between you and management as you get settled into the job. In one of these meetings, probably three to six months into the job, begin to talk with your boss about skill improvement. Let him know you are committed to your job and to making a difference with your presence in the department. To do this, you need to make three points:

1. I want to make a place for myself here, and to do that I need to be the best I can be.

2. I'd like to hear any suggestions you have on skills that would make me more valuable to the team.

3. These are skill sets I see as important in doing a stellar job, and I'd like to develop them by doing _____ [*itemize the assignments that would develop these areas*].

Your boss will make suggestions, and you should react positively to them. Lay out a plan of action with realizable, step-by-step goals. Implement the advice, and follow up informally every six to eight weeks to communicate both your commitment and progress; this establishes credibility and visibility where it counts. Do this and, apart from improving your professional competencies, you will have marked yourself out as someone who thinks, cares, and makes things happen. It's the first step in turning your boss into an ally.

Make Your Boss Your Ally

There is no such thing as a dead-end job, so give this opportunity everything you have. Employers notice who is working hard and who is there for a paycheck and a job.

Marshall J. Karp, MA, NCC, LPC, Career Counselor, *www.marshalljkarp.com*

Your boss has a profound influence over your ability to climb the ladder at the new company and build a successful career; you can help this happen by making your boss a fan and ally:

- Understand what's needed and deliver it on time and in the way your boss prefers.
- Make sure your work is accurate and what is requested rather than what you can get away with.
- Seek advice and accept constructive criticism gracefully.
- Share the credit you receive for work well done.

- Communicate clearly, professionally, honestly, and as often as your boss wants.
- Be a reliable team member in thought, word, and deed.
- Become *the most* reliable team member in thought, word, and deed, and you become a leader.
- Consistently make your boss look good to others through your words and deeds.
- Thank your boss for either specific support or general encouragement.
- Never assume a job is complete when you hand it in. Be prepared to revise, edit, or recast your work.
- Increase your skills and expand your connectivity by volunteering for any interdepartmental projects or committees.
- Look for orphan projects that no one wants but that need to be done.

Avoid doing the following:

- Don't overcommit yourself to special projects to the point that your performance suffers.
- Never display disloyalty. If you're seeking a promotion, your boss should know and be part of the program.
- Ensure by your actions that others within your department know of your loyalty to them and to the department's goals. Never criticize your boss to other employees.
- Don't be a doomsayer: No one wants to listen to the employee who's predicting the imminent collapse of civilization. Even if the company or the industry is experiencing some difficult times, be a positive influence. This doesn't mean you should stick your head in the sand and get caught job hunting with three hundred of your closest colleagues: You make decisions based on MeInc's long-term goals, but no one else needs or has a right to know about MeInc's business plans.
- Too often departments take refuge in a narrow separatism that counterpoises their interests to everyone else's. Sales says, "Those

people in Accounting are obstructionist bean-counters who get in the way of the people who bring in the money," while the accountants say, "Sales are a bunch of wild-eyed maniacs who don't understand the practical realities; it's our work that ensures the paychecks don't bounce."

Don't buy into this mindset. Instead, respect and show interest in the roles others play in the complex machinery that helps a company achieve success; this will increase your credibility and visibility, your networks, and your frame of reference for how the moneymaking machinery of business works.

Together, these attitudes and actions will cement a good relationship with your boss and could well lead to your boss also becoming your mentor, personally involved in your growth and success.

Developing Mentors

> There is no such thing as job security, but top performers get closest. They attract followers and mentors; they develop mutual respect and important liaisons with decision-makers.
>
> **Valentino B. Martinez,** President, *www.managementconsultants.us*

Mentor-acolyte relationships have been an integral part of successful careers throughout the ages. Mentors are usually more experienced professionals whom you admire, from whom you can learn, and who you feel can accelerate your professional growth in some way. Remember:

- Mentors aren't like lovers. You can have more than one at a time.
- Although age and wisdom don't always go together, it is better to find a mentor older than you, because they'll have skills you don't and the wisdom of greater experience. You need both.
- Mentor-acolyte relationships can introduce you to your mentor's network.

- Look for mentors both within and without your area of subject-matter expertise, both within your company and in the larger pond of your local professional community.
- Let the relationship develop naturally, over time. You might work together, have known each other, and get on well for some time before you say, "I want to learn everything you know. I want you to teach me, and in return I will stand at your side, have your back, and do anything I can to return this favor."

You can *become* a mentor, too. Technology savvy is pretty much second nature to you, and you can use this to your advantage by leveraging your computer skills to help people who are otherwise your professional superiors. Look for opportunities to help your seniors and then do so *very* quietly and confidentially and you will be rewarded with valuable relationships.

The Vacuum Theory of Professional Growth

Opportunities for professional growth come in many guises, and most of them come disguised as problems that everyone tries to avoid with a shrug and a "That's not in my job description, babycakes." By working on your *technical* and *transferable skills* and making the *professional values* a vibrant part of your *professional self* in the ways we've discussed, you have positioned yourself to notice the problem issues that everyone else is avoiding like the plague. Many of these you will want to steer clear of too, but some of them might offer real opportunities for differentiating yourself.

> Be the person who is known for "getting things done—period."
> While your peers are pointing out the obstacles, seek out the opportunities. Sometimes they are difficult to see, but rest assured, they exist.
>
> **Kevin Kermes,** Founder, *www.careerattraction.com*

A former boss of mine applied something I've come to call the Vacuum Theory of Growth: Walking down the hall one day, he saw a gum wrapper on the floor. He bent and picked it up. "Only two people would do that: the janitor and maybe the president. They both know who I am," he said, smiling.

This guy executed his job with utter excellence; he volunteered for and was involved in every initiative for growth that the company had going, was always one of the first three people in the office, and would smilingly lend a hand to anyone who needed it. He also looked for vacuums, necessary jobs that no one wanted to do. Consequently, he had allies everywhere and at every level, and he always knew everything that happened in the company before it happened.

Once you are more than adequately competent in the essential *technical skills* of your job, look around for opportunity. Then start sucking up extra responsibility by doing those necessary, extra things that no one else wants to do because it's "not my job." The result is enhanced credibility, visibility with the people who count, and a power base for future growth. When you do the right things for the right reasons, you always benefit from the effort; sometimes not immediately, but you always do benefit.

Vacuum theory is an expression of motivation: do your job well first, then help others whenever and however you can; do the jobs others won't and make a visible difference with your presence every day.

Making the Inner Circle and Establishing a Desirable Brand

Every profession, every company, and every department has an inner circle. As a recent graduate, you will look to identify how this works in your department and company in the first few months of your tenure. You'll gradually come to notice the people who have real influence and the people who don't, because just as there is an inner circle, there is an outer circle too; you can join either, it's up to you. The inner circle is where your job is safest and where the plum assignments, raises, and promotions live. *It's where you become visible to the power players two, three, and four levels above you.* Add the following five commitments to everything you have learned so far and you will gain the attention of, and acceptance by, the people who make up the inner circles within your department and company.

1. Secure your job and establish a sound foundation for skill development.
2. Work to become an accepted *team member* in the ways suggested.
3. Commit to the success of every project, every team, and every department with which you are involved.
4. Get behind every project leader, no matter who it is and what your relationship is with her up to this point. You will be called upon to work for peer project leaders, when you might feel better qualified. Nevertheless, you work to make both the project and that project leader a success. This is *teamwork*, and if you hope to become a *leader* you must first be a *team player*—remember, a leader is simply a team-player position on a higher-level team. Don't worry about your work getting overlooked; *the people who matter to your professional growth always notice your efforts.*
5. Give your best on every assignment, no matter how undesirable, because you know that taking the rough with the smooth is part of achieving success. *The real players, the members of the inner circle, know this and respect it in others.*

People who get promoted have "street smarts." They interact well with others at all levels of the organization. They have the ability to get things done quickly, efficiently, and on time. It's better to be 95 percent accurate and get it done on time versus being perfect, but a day late.

Rich Grant, Director of Career Services, *www.thomas.edu*

When you polish your *technical skills*, support every task you tackle with *transferable skills*, and make judgments grounded in sound *professional values*, you become a highly desirable employee. When you pursue your work with *commitment* and *enlightened self-interest*, you will slowly and quietly be welcomed into the inner circle of your department and then your company.

Inner Circles Beyond Your Company

Build on these foundations to evolve into the consummate professional you want to be and be seen as, and you will begin to manifest a desirable professional brand.

This brand grows over time, first in your department and then company-wide. Then, when you become involved with your professional community by joining the local chapter of a professional association, you begin to take this brand into a larger arena. The people you meet through a professional association are *the most committed and best-connected people in your professional world. They usually belong to the inner circles of their own companies, and probably have the key to some of your strategic career moves over the years.*

Membership and active involvement in professional associations is the smartest career strategy you can initiate to achieve wide professional connectivity. You will keep current with industry issues and new skills, and you will get to know and be known by everyone who is anyone in your profession. Make involvement in association activities something you do as a matter of course every month.

How to Pursue and Win a Promotion

The work on your first promotion starts when you join the company. Spend the first few months figuring out the way things work. Once you understand the culture, get up to speed with all your job's deliverables, and know who's who in your department and why, it's time to start strategizing your first step up the promotional ladder. This doesn't often happen in the first few months; it rarely happens in a year, and for most people, significant promotions often don't happen till the second or third year.

Your next step up the ladder doesn't come automatically as a result of being in the inner circle, but it positions you to make that step. Promotions come as a result of hard work, credibility, visibility, and a plan of attack. *You get hired based on credentials, not potential,* and *you get promoted when you are a known quantity* within the company.

This is how you win promotions:

1. First, secure the job you have by becoming the best you can be and the best there is at this job in your company. It can help to review your *TJD* work and the formal job description for this job. Then add the skills experience is showing that you need. Do you have superior skills in all the areas required for this job? This skill development secures your job, increases your employability, and shows management that you are someone who is self-directed and capable of professional growth.

2. When you are ready, identify the next logical step up your chosen professional ladder, collect six to ten job postings for your target job title, and do a new *TJD* on that target job.

3. Execute a GAP analysis on the new job's requirements. Identify the *gaps* between the skills you have and the skills you need to qualify you for that next job. Flagging missing skills and experience gives you a *professional development program* to pursue.

4. Identify ways you can build these skills within company activities and on your own initiative.

5. Talk to your boss about your desire to gain these new skills and experience. Explain that you want to work towards this job over time by developing the skills it demands.

6. Model yourself on people who do this job successfully. Look for a mentor who is doing this job. Ask how they got there and the other social networking questions you asked to get an insider view of the job you just landed.

Moving Up

When a position opens up, a company normally looks within and then goes outside for talent. It is easier to climb the ladder within a company where you are a known quantity and have the kind of sterling reputation you have worked to achieve. You will throw your hat in the ring when opportunities arise and be patient if you don't win first time out.

However, sometimes your capabilities won't be as well known as you imagined, because sometimes you can get stereotyped and pigeonholed; if so, you will need to make a formal argument for your qualifications.

Candidates from outside the company come armed with resumes that carefully focus on the experience and abilities they can bring to the job. You should prepare in the same way, first creating a resume targeted on this job and then preparing for interviews just as you would with another company.

Submit your resume for consideration either to your manager or to HR; having a properly prepared resume encourages your employers to look at you in this new light and tells them that you have the qualifications and a serious desire for greater responsibility. If you have established yourself as a valuable employee, this and the fact that you have a kick-ass resume prepared will encourage them to take your candidacy seriously.

When It's Time to Make a Strategic Career Move

However, despite teamwork, patience, and dedication to doing a good job, a time may come when you believe this next step is not possible with your current company. If this step is important to getting what you want from life, then the time might have arrived when you need to very quietly plan the next step in your career.

I encourage you to be patient. Growth is always slower than you expect and the good news of your absolute wonderfulness is slower to travel than you might expect; besides, you have to consider the possibility that you aren't quite as good as you think you are yet. On top of this, many of the people who climb the highest on the ladder of success are people who have found a good company and played the long game, waiting patiently for growth opportunities. These people have employment records that show an employment tenure with individual companies far exceeding the average four years.

That said, if you have plans for professional growth and you have been with the company three or more years without significant increases and/or changes in responsibility reflected by title change and salary increases, it may well be time to consider a strategic career move.

When this day dawns, you are armed with greatly enhanced skills and the professional credibility and visibility that now constitute a truly valid *professional brand*. You don't piss this away at the first opportunity. You organize, research, and plan the strategies that will deliver your next move and give you the widest possible choice of opportunity.

By this time you should have mature and vibrant networks online and with alumni groups and be an active member of at least your regional professional community. You have a resume targeted to the next target job, and you have developed the skills and experience to excel—so you have the credentials. Plus you have a database of companies and contacts within them that you established in your first job search and added to while on this first job. Pulling all this together, you have the time, tools, skills, connections, and knowledge to make this first strategic career move on your own timetable.

RESOURCES *Knock 'em Dead Breaking Into Management* and *Knock 'em Dead Professional Communication* are both available at *www.knockemdead.com*.

CHAPTER 14

CHANGING JOBS, CHANGING CAREERS

As you now know, the surest path to that elusive American dream of a home, a family, and disposable income is the pursuit of a *core career*. We discussed the choice of career with reference to the health and size of the industry and the jobs you are likely to pursue within it. These considerations have vital implications for job security and the ability to find another job in times of economic upheaval.

> Try to align your interests and skills with a career. Whatever your interest is, there is a career attached to it! Try doing a Google search with the name of your interest and the word "careers."
>
> **Leslie Zaikis,** Director of Business Development, *www.levoleague.com*

Job change happens—sometimes planned, sometimes not—and it is rarely easy. But you don't have to be caught unawares by a layoff. You can become more informed, better connected, and plan your moves. With a career-management database in place and relevant social networks developed, the moves can be made on a considered basis and at a time of your choosing, whether you decide there is no further opportunity to move toward your goals with a current employer, or outside forces tell you that your job is no longer secure. It takes careful planning and execution to keep the cash flow uninterrupted, but you now have the awareness and the tools in hand to execute strategic career moves within your chosen profession.

The Probability of Career Change in Your Life

> You WILL change careers, perhaps several times in your life, so develop your transferable skills—like your skin, they go where you go.
>
> **Mark Babbitt,** CEO and Founder, *www.youtern.com*

We also discussed the probability that you might well need to change your core career a couple of times. Sticking with the same job and switching employers is tough enough, but it pales in comparison to changing careers in the midst of your work life. Changing careers takes careful thought and planning if you want to avoid major economic dislocation. While I don't recommend making a career change during a recession, we are a huge economy and there are plenty of jobs out there, and when you go about it with the right preparation and determination, you can succeed.

The Challenges of Career Change

A career change is a much more intimidating affair than a job change within your chosen profession, because it can cause extensive financial and emotional dislocation unless unfailingly planned in advance. The worst time to change careers is when you are out of work: If you get caught unawares and without options in an economic downturn, you can get short of cash while the bills are piling nose-high. When you change careers, you are changing the way you make your living, so the competition is fiercer than you have ever faced: You are up against fresh young grads who are probably cheaper, or candidates who already have experience in that profession.

> A career change that is based on emotions is never advisable, while one that is the result of careful thought and self-reflection has a greater potential of being successful.
>
> **Sultan Camp,** Military Transition and Social Network Specialist, *www.zeiders.com*

It is wiser to plan career change well ahead of time and make the shift when the economy is good and there are more job opportunities than candidates. If you begin to anticipate the need for career change—and the farther in advance the better—yet you are not certain of the new career you want to pursue, you can refer to the discussion in Chapter 1 on career choice for help with researching and deciding on a sensible new career path, and remember the database at *www.knockemdead.com* that allows you to match careers with degrees. It can help you evaluate options for the degree you already have or, if you are considering getting another degree, the jobs people usually get with that degree.

Identify Skills and Credentials You Need to Make the Transition

> Identify any education/training credentials and consider options for securing them before you make your move. When you initiate the change, make sure anything you have done to brand yourself online and offline is adapted to support your new career direction.
>
> **Chris Perry,** Brand and Marketing Generator, *www.careerrocketeer.com*

Once you have decided on a career change, you have to decide the profession you want to pursue and the industry in which you will pursue it. Then you can really start to put your plan into motion by deciding on a target job title and executing a Target Job Deconstruction exercise to understand who and what employers look for when they hire someone to do this job. With this new *TJD*, identify the skills and credentials you need to have to increase the odds of a successful career change, then go about acquiring them.

Overcoming Obstacles with a Career Change

I recently helped a guy having problems with a mid-career shift. In his late thirties, thirteen unhappy years in sales/marketing had led to career reappraisal and a subsequent return to university to gain a Finance MBA.

His job search was bogged down and he diagnosed the problem as, "no job offers because of my inability to answer specific questions about *why the career change*." I told him getting his new career moving would take more than a few snappy answers to tough interview questions. In fact his problems stemmed from a combination of factors.

It wasn't that he hadn't yet latched onto the most convincing arguments to justify his career shift. The more important causes for rejection of his candidacy stemmed from:

- His lack of understanding, believing, and demonstrating that he understood the deliverables of the target job and its role within the department
- His lack of understanding of how the new profession and industry worked and why it functioned the way it did
- His lack of understanding of why his prior professional experience was actually a distinct benefit to the new employer

What did he need to focus his attention on before attempting to make a dramatic career change? He had to develop a deep understanding of this new job where he was going to spend the majority of his waking hours; he had to learn where there was connectivity between his old career and the new one, and where there was no connectivity, he had to show a deep understanding of the deliverables of the job and the problems he would be anticipating, preventing when he could, and solving when prevention was not possible. With this approach he could build bridges of connectivity between his old job and this new one, bridges that would enable the employer to say, "Sure, you can walk on over."

Take career change one step at a time. If you're an accountant who wants to be a graphic designer, look for a new job as an accountant with a graphic design company. Then build the skills and you're halfway there.

Leslie Ayres, Job Search Guru, *www.thejobsearchguru.com*

Understanding the New Job, Profession, and Industry

Your success at landing job interviews and then acing them in a career-change job search will dramatically improve with greater understanding of your target job's function and the world it inhabits. Your current job and your target job in the new profession and industry have two things in common:

1. They both exist to perform a specialized function that is a *small cog in the complex moneymaking machinery* that is a corporation.
2. They both exist to *anticipate, prevent, and solve problems* in an area of specific technical expertise within a department of similarly focused professionals.

To understand what employers in this new profession are looking for, think about this new job's deliverables, the problems it is there to prevent and solve, and how it contributes to the larger goals of the department and ultimately the company's profitability. In short, *it's everything you learned in researching your first target job* applied to the new target profession and industry sector.

Do the research. Ask questions. Join the professional networking groups around your new career. Shadow someone in that target job. Immerse yourself in the new professional community and build a network.

Amanda Pouchot, Founder, *www.levoleague.com*

Use Your Networks

As soon as you determine on a new direction, start building networks within that profession that can help you make the transition. The people who can help you most are the same high-value job titles you will need to develop for networking and job search when you start pursuing the new job. Reach out to people who hold the job title(s) that you will be pursuing, as well as the people who hold job titles one, two, and three levels above it.

The contacts you make in the new industry can tell you about the role of the job in contributing to profitability, the problems it exists to solve, and its role within the department. They can tell you about the *technical skills* required and how they are applied in the work. They can also tell you which *transferable skills* and *professional values* are most important in that job and how they are applied. For example, *multitasking* will naturally be an important skill. But what are the primary activities of the new job, and when do they occur during the working day? And what other important but repetitive activities must also be scheduled and completed during the working week?

Your best bet for learning more about the day-to-day challenges of a target job in a new profession is to talk with people working in the desired area within the target industry/profession—*people with similar educational and work backgrounds, ideally people who have already made a similar shift successfully* and who hold, have held, or whose jobs require them to work with, your target job title. If you are a member of LinkedIn, you can execute searches to identify these people. Your alumni association and other social and community networks will also be a useful resource, as will a professional association related to the new job. With all these resources, you can search for members:

- Working in the target profession
- Working in the target profession and sharing a similar educational background
- Working in the target profession and having made a similar transition

Apart from people who share your transitional experience from one profession to another, people up and down the promotional ladder in that job (the high-value networking titles) and profession can all offer worthwhile advice.

With networking contacts who have made a similar transition, you will want answers to the following:

- How has your prior professional background paid off in your new profession?
- How has it helped you better understand _____ to the benefit of the corporation?
- What special insights have you gained that made you more productive?
- How did you make the transition?
- Why do you think this combined background of _____ and _____ is helpful to an employer?

Especially useful will be the advice you receive from network contacts who share a common background about how the target job fits into the department and contributes to the company's bottom line.

> Think about doing an internship in your off-hours to make sure you enjoy the work. When you know this career path is right for you, the most important thing is to build a relevant network.
>
> **Josh Tolan**, CEO, *www.sparkhire.com*

It will take time to make the contacts and gather the insights you need to fully understand the target job in its day-to-day professional context. The knowledge you gather will help you build the bridges that connect your past experience with your new direction and the ability to lead your interviewers across those bridges.

It's Your Resume, Stupid

You cannot simply update your existing resume when you are making a career change. Resumes not only open doors for you, they give the employer a focus and road map for the interview; in a very real way, *the understanding of your target job expressed in your resume sets the tone for the interview.* You started with a *TJD* of the new target job, developed the skills the new job and profession require, and researched what the true role and deliverables of the job are. Now, with a complete understanding of the job, you can build a resume better focused on those deliverables. This will help you land interviews and dramatically increase your odds of turning them into job offers.

Job Search Tactics

A job search involving a career change takes longer than a regular job search, because it requires research and networking to understand the job, time for skill and credential development and job-search coordination, and the even longer time needed to win a job offer in the new field. Implementation of your job search should follow the plan of attack laid out earlier and should feature an emphasis on direct research and high value–title networking.

When your job search involves career change, winning a job offer will never depend on the answers to a handful of interview questions; it will depend on your ability to communicate your understanding of the target job's deliverables, *why* and *how* you can deliver on them, and how your prior experience has relevance in this new world. All of this is possible with the steps we have discussed in this chapter.

CHAPTER 15

LIFETIME CAREER-MANAGEMENT STRATEGIES

You have been taught to think of career management as choosing one thing you can do and settling down to it for a lifetime. You hang on with ten fingers and ten toes, and if you should lose one of them, well golly-gosh you hang on with nine, because that's the way it's done. Your loyalty will be rewarded with job and financial security and steady professional growth. This delightful fairy tale ends with a comfortable retirement, featuring a home you own and a cabin at the lake with a boat bobbing lazily at the end of the dock.

Despite this being a pile of rocking-horse droppings, career strategists have done nothing to replace it with a more viable model. As people have lost jobs and professions have vanished because of technological change and economic recession, the supposedly cutting-edge career advice continues to be that change happens, change is for the best, and "Bless your heart, we're getting rid of these stinky old jobs and replacing them with bright shiny new ones." Now all you have to do is choose one *other* thing you can do, settle down again for the rest of your life, and hang on with your nine remaining fingers. And if you lose one of those, well . . .

In the past thirty years technology has changed every facet of the way we live our lives and do our jobs. In such a turbulent world of work, the traditional approach to career management of one career forever, unless it disappears, followed by another "one career forever" no longer makes sense. I have been working in career management for more than thirty years; I have seen the change happening, I have seen how this change dislocates and derails people's lives, and I have spent these decades slowly defining new approaches to the issues of long-term career management—approaches that recognize the uncertainty of the world of work you are about to enter and the total implausibility of the head-in-the-sand approach to professional development that you have been brought up to believe in. Today, the concept of one career and one job is a recipe for disaster. Change will be the only constant in your career, and you can either figure out a way to get out in front of this uncertainty, or you can sink into despair and eventual unemployability.

Don't sputter along from job to job and career to career, with all the attendant financial dislocation and soul-wrenching self-doubt. Learn how to carve a path to sustainable employability. You can do it.

The New Career Management

As a nation, we typically start to work in our teens and retire around the age of sixty-five, although your parents' generation knows this will not be economically feasible because of the effect regular and increasingly violent economic swings have had on retirement plans. This picture of financial insecurity isn't likely to improve, especially while corporate and political greed blithely sanctions the outsourcing and wage depression that enrich the wealthiest 1 percent, who still manage to convince a plurality of Americans that all 99 percent of them are just a little elbow grease away from owning a private jet, and that therefore it's in their best interest to support no taxes for corporations and lower taxes for the rich.

The reality you face is that employment unpredictability will continue to threaten your ability to get what you want out of life if you follow the traditional "one life, one career" paradigm. You need to embrace a new approach to lifetime career management. You have already started down this path by internalizing the MeInc frame of mind that has informed every page of *Knock 'em Dead: Secrets & Strategies for First-Time Job Seekers*: a more businesslike approach to managing your professional affairs, an approach that teaches you how to do everything possible to succeed in your chosen *core career*, yet focuses on what is best for your own economic survival, prosperity, and fulfillment.

Where Do You Want to Be at Retirement?

Don't dismiss this question just because you're at the start of your work life. The most productive way to get what you want out of life is to start thinking about your endgame *now*: where you want to be and what you want your life to be like twenty years down the road (your foreseeable future and the period in which the arc of the rest of your life will largely be determined). Your life goals for the next two decades—which will go by in a flash—have to go beyond fine dining and a glossy magazine's description of the ideal consumer. You need to think deeply about the quality and meaning of the life you want, about the practical approaches to making a living, and also about what gives you joy and what you would like to do if only you had the time to make it work. Once you can define where you are going and what you want, you can begin to structure a plan of attack that will deliver your dreams.

> There's a delicate balance in life between following your passions and paying your dues; sometimes one is necessary to achieve the other. Get to know people who are where you want to be in one, five, and ten years, and be realistic: No career is as glamorous as it seems from the outside.
>
> **Kathryn Minshew,** Founder and CEO, *www.thedailymuse.com*

You can get most places in life that you want to reach, so long as you have a clear picture of where you stand today and where you want to stand tomorrow or twenty years down the road. Once you have articulated a goal, you can work backward, defining the steps you will need to take to reach it. When this is done, you will have stepping-stones that will take you down you the path you want to follow.

Everything in your understanding of career management to date has centered on finding one thing you can do and doing nothing but that one thing, forever . . . could anything be worse? This is why we have generations of adults whose sense of self is entirely defined by their *core career* job title. Your life need not follow this outmoded construct.

You have a dozen ideas in your head about the things you want to do with your life, but you think they're mutually exclusive and you can only choose one of them. I'm telling you this is wrong; in fact, far from being in conflict, most of your dreams are complementary. You can dream of being the president of the company, a surgeon, a lawyer, or a teacher, *and* of becoming the president of your own company, *and* of becoming an artist, writer, or musician. This is not an either/or world anymore, and there are ways to bring such multifaceted dreams to life.

The Building Blocks for Success and Personal Fulfillment in an Uncertain World

There are three paths to building a successful life for yourself:

1. **Core Career:** Building a career working for companies that pay a salary and offer vacations, benefits, and some degree of professional growth.
   - *Core Career Reality:* There is no real job security, but it is still the most secure route to middle-class success.
2. **Entrepreneurial Career:** When you work for yourself, there's no employer between you and the money. The closer you get to the source of money, to bringing it steadily in your own front door, the closer you are to economic security and real freedom in your life.
   - *Entrepreneurial Career Reality:* More businesses fail than succeed. Most entrepreneurs rush into a business without preparation or skills, and give up their entrepreneurial

dreams after that first failure. Almost all successful entrepreneurs have experienced one or more failures before they achieve success.

Your entrepreneurial dreams need not include building a full-time business. They might embrace the pursuit of a part-time business that you enjoy, which delivers an additional income stream.

3. **Dream Career:** It can be anything you want, from writing the Great American Novel to becoming a cellist in the Vienna Philharmonic.

   - *Dream Career Reality:* A dream career should be something that gives you joy, *puts the juice back in your life.* By definition hard to achieve, it should not replace a steady means of making a living; besides, that *core career* has all kinds of valuable lessons that will help you realize your dreams. If you hope to live that dream, you have to turn it into achievable goals and a plan of action: actual steps you can take every day that steadily move you ever closer to bringing that dream to reality.

   Everything starts with a dream, and stays that way over the time it takes you to work steadily toward it. This can take many years; for example, I have been a writer for twenty-seven years now, but I worked at it nights and weekends for twenty years, from the age of fifteen to thirty-five, before I could make a living at it. Meanwhile I pursued a successful *core career* and failed with two entrepreneurial endeavors.

   Your *dream career* ceases being a dream the moment you start to make money from it. At that moment you become a creative entrepreneur, and your *dream career* transforms into an *entrepreneurial career.* It happens, and if you are the creative type, which all entrepreneurs and business people are, you'll soon latch onto *another* dream, knowing you crave the juice that having dreams and pursuing them brings to your life.

There's a Life Waiting Beyond Your Core Career

With all its uncertainties, your *core career* is still the surest path to security and success, and while it shouldn't be your only path in such an insecure world, there is a trade-off: Use your day-to-day *core career* experience wisely and you will find that it can be a complete educational program for the launch of successful *dream* and *entrepreneurial careers*.

The value of the *transferable skills* has long been accepted in the professional world, but until the 1990s no one had ever looked at their role in the success of entrepreneurial and creative endeavors. In 1995, I published a book about people who achieve success by breaking the rules. To write it, I funded a study by behavioral psychologists that looked at the *skills and values* needed for long-term career success in *core, dream,* and *entrepreneurial* careers. As I said, there was already consensus in the professional community on the group of *transferable skills* and *professional values* that led to success in a *core career*, but no comparative studies for *core* versus *entrepreneurial* versus *dream careers*.

The big question was: What are the underlying skills needed for success in these different fields of endeavor? Are they different or do they overlap? The study was managed by Dr. David Caruso, a behavioral psychologist, with academic oversight from the psychology department at the University of New Hampshire.

The study determined that there are a handful of skills that increase the odds of success *in all three career paths*. These *skills* and *values* had been accepted as important to success in the professional world, and I'd been writing about their application in pursuit of a successful *core career* for years, but no one had ever looked at what it took to be financially viable as an entrepreneur or in creative endeavors.

This groundbreaking work was roundly condemned on TV and radio stations across the nation because—get this—*I was suggesting Americans be disloyal to their employers!* I was therefore at best un-American and quite possibly a communist! It was all very well to help people develop the *transferable skills* and *professional values* needed to succeed in a **core** *career*—a career in which *someone else* controls the money and tells you where to go, what to do, and how to do it—but to encourage the same skill development in the service of *entrepreneurial* and *dream careers*? That would suggest that people ought to care more about their own success than the success of the corporation. Scandalous!

While I was studying and writing about the universal applicability of the *transferable skills* and *professional values* to *entrepreneurial* and *dream* as well as *core careers*, I was demonstrating that thesis in my own life. I had turned my *dream career* of writing into a *core career*, but now I had other dreams. I applied the *transferable skills* in developing and receiving two optical patents for a photographic accessory that eradicated the red-eye in photographs. Developed with a neighbor and friend and bought by the Western Television company, *Redx* was then sold on TV: "1-800, not available in stores, etc." We did this at nights and on weekends, and we both had full-time jobs and young families to raise. If we had lacked a single one of the *transferable skills*, it simply would not have happened. The same *transferable skills* and *professional values* that had led to success in our *core careers* were now giving birth to *entrepreneurial success*. Almost everyone you can think of who owns a company, is an entrepreneur, is successful in the arts, or otherwise has control of their lives, broke out by investing themselves in their lives in the same way.

How to Get What You Want Out of Life

Envision the life you want, seek it out, and make it happen. The people in this world who make the biggest difference, and who have the most fun in the process, are the people who are courageous enough to be real and live full-out.

Leslie Ayres, Job Search Guru, *www.thejobsearchguru.com*

You have dreams? You have goals? You have passions? The key to bringing them to life is fostering the *transferable skills* and *professional values*, securing a *core career*, and working steadily toward them. Even if you don't achieve all your dreams, the worst that can happen is you polish your *transferable skills* and *professional values* and therefore increase your employability and potential for promotions and raises in your *core career*.

This should make you look at the *transferable skills* and your *core career* in a new light.

Applying the *transferable skills* and *professional values* every day will:

- Encourage success in every deliverable of your job
- Increase your job security
- Mark you for special assignments
- Build the foundation for a desirable *professional brand*
- Speed your acceptance to the inner circles of your professional world
- Develop the underlying skills you need for *entrepreneurial* success
- Develop the underlying skills you need for *dream career*/creative success

Your *core career* gives you the best odds of achieving success and the American dream of a home and disposable income. If you have dreams of entrepreneurial and creative success, these same *core career* jobs can be your training ground, full of OJT (on-the-job-training) opportunities to learn the lessons of business and apply them to your own pursuits, your own enlightened self-interest.

It's Good to Have Goals in Life— Beyond Becoming a CPA

Graduation from school forces you to face the realities of finally entering an adult world that has one overwhelming message: grow up. At the same time tens of thousands of parents are telling their offspring, "Get serious, stop messing around and wasting your time." One of two things happens:

1. Some people take their dreams, fold them neatly, and stick them under the bed along with much of the joy they get from life. This forever diminishes them.

2. Some people rebel, refuse a professional path and pursue their crazy dreams. Without objectivity, understanding, or possessing the skills that bring dreams to life, they believe all that crap about "pursuing your bliss." Ninety-nine percent of them fail, by which time it is too late to get on track with a professional career. These people's economic opportunities are forever stunted.

The more viable option is not to put your dreams in a box under the bed or to tilt at windmills like a crazy person, but to make your dreams of success, of making your life meaningful, of getting what you want out of life, an integral part of your life. Own them, make them part of the MeInc mission, and invest yourself in the beliefs and activities that over time will bring them to life.

The more complete your vision of the future, the more clearly you can identify and define the many small steps, taken day-by-day, that will bring you toward your goals. Meaningful alternate pathways to success and personal fulfillment represent long-term commitments that probably won't spring into bloom this first year of your professional life. It is important you understand this—instant success very rarely happens except on television. Your *entrepreneurial* and *dream* pursuits can take years to bear fruit, but their pursuit will enrich your life in the process.

What You Want Out of Life Will Change

Your wants, needs, and dreams will change as the years pass. Some of the pursuits that seem worthwhile and energizing now will likely be replaced with new passions in your thirties, and then again in your forties and so on. Most people who attempt to pursue their dreams try once in their teens and twenties and, failing, decide they are failures and vow never to make the same mistake again. However, the people who break out, who become successful in less traditional ways, take their knocks, own their mistakes, lick their wounds, and learn to do better next time; and there always *is* a next time until they achieve success. *They simply don't quit,* no matter how long it takes.

If you commit to a plan of action for pursuing simultaneous career paths, learn from your mistakes, and commit yourself to achieving your dreams no matter how long it takes, that crazy idea that didn't work out in your teens or twenties shouldn't prevent you from trying again in your thirties with a new idea, or in your forties, fifties, and beyond. Henry Dow, the founder of Dow Chemical, the largest chemical company in the world, failed five times before he made his dream work; Laura Ingalls Wilder, the author of *Little House on the Prairie,* didn't start writing until she was sixty-five years old; and my friend Ross, who drew Mickey Mouse for Disney and is one of the last living animators who worked on *Fantasia* back in the 1930s, is completely engaged in a new philanthropic business venture at ninety-two. When you plan for multiple parallel career paths, you are committing to a complete approach to life. You are committing to being engaged in life rather than watching it whizz by on a screen.

A Successful Career Is Not a Sprint

A successful career is a marathon, not a sprint, so whatever your goals, the sooner you start toward them the better. *It is okay to have multiple goals in life,* because if you buy into this approach, *you have the tools to bring them to life, and you have the time if you have the commitment and* **start today***.*

Do it, because you *can* do it and you have the time. If you don't have time, I can give you, right now, a gift of five hours every day to invest in making your life a richer experience: Stop watching TV. Yup, that's how much TV the average American watches, and you're probably not an exception. Stop watching your life whiz by on the screen, stop training to be a good consumer and an obedient drone. Instead, invest some or all of that time in you—*in your life*—in MeInc and the realization of your dreams.

Look for stepping-stones to take you from where you stand today to where you want to stand tomorrow; and look for connectivity between how the actions that can help you achieve goals in your new corporate *core career* might also encourage the steps you take toward an *entrepreneurial* or *dream career.*

Stepping-Stones and Calendars

I once knew a young man who worked as a headhunter—not a very glamorous job at the time. He was relatively successful but unfulfilled (he dreamed of being a writer or an actor). He wanted to change careers but had to keep paying the bills. What did he do? He looked for stepping-stones to get away from the front line of sales. After some thought, he decided that becoming a sales trainer looked like a promising option, so he started to help get new sales employees up-to-speed with his current employer.

Planning Strategic Career Moves

He used what he already had—*technical skills* and an ability to share his knowledge (*teamwork* and *communication skills*)—as stepping-stones to get where he wanted to go. Becoming a trainer would get him off the front line of sales into another area of professional expertise and give him new *technical skills* to transfer from company to company and even from industry to industry. Plus the training work would have him up and performing in front of an audience, helping his stage presence as an actor (and increasing his credibility and visibility*).*

Skill Development

He worked hard and long to develop good training skills, and he always looked for connectivity between his *core career* goals and his dream of one day writing the Great American Novel and never working another day in his life. The more he understood the mechanics of professional success, the more he saw patterns emerge; and the more connectivity he found between seemingly disparate activities, the more opportunities he saw for himself. For example, he saw the absence of training manuals (*creativity* based on *technical skills* and being a *team player*) and how they could increase productivity with new employees.

He wanted to be a novelist, and knew from his studies (*commitment, determination*) that any writing would help in learning how to craft powerful sentences. So he wrote any manual, any time, for any employer he worked for (*communication skills*). It served multiple career goals:

- It branded him as someone thoroughly *committed.*
- It branded him as someone with a special sauce to bring to the table.
- It increased his professional credibility.
- It increased his visibility by widening his contacts and sphere of influence.
- It brought him into relationships with people he otherwise wouldn't know.
- It developed his *writing* skills.

Stepping-Stones

Two jobs, many manuals, and almost seven years later, he landed with a franchisor of employment service companies as a sales and management trainer. Committed to succeeding, he continued to learn everything he could about his profession as a trainer (*technical skills*) and about the world of employment. He found a great mentor and helped the mentor in return.

Within a year he was being recruited for other franchise companies in other industries (*brand recognition*); but he stayed and shortly became Director of Training and Development as his boss moved up to VP (*inner circle*). Over the years he had built career stepping-stones for himself, using a horizontally oriented career that could cross industry lines (more security and more opportunities for *professional growth*).

It Takes Time

Stepping-stones take you from where you are to where you want to be, but it takes time. This young man had bills to pay and now a family coming along but he still dreamed of being a novelist or an actor (*dream careers*). He wasn't either, but he'd moved toward both in an organized and committed manner, while he pursued a successful *core career*. He was very good at his job and had polished his writing and performance skills along the way. He was indeed much happier, more secure, and more successful.

This young man had other dreams too. He dreamed of working for himself. He'd tried three times before but the dreams hadn't worked out (*entrepreneurial, determination*). As a trainer, part of his job was *writing* training manuals; what was a *dream* avocation had grown into a *core career technical skill*. He wrote dozens of manuals to hone his writing skills (*professional development program*), and he wrote novels as he sat in airports or hotels on business trips (*multitasking* and *communication*). He got a book published five years after starting this new approach to life and career management, but twenty years after he'd first thought of himself as wanting to be a writer (*dream career* becomes *entrepreneurial career*). Now, twenty-seven years later, he's written sixteen books that are published and acclaimed around the world, has his own company, and is still nowhere near finished. Over time, pursuit of those *dreams* enriched his *core career* skills and employability; after twenty years' pursuit, they started making money and gave birth to a real *entrepreneurial career* that became a stable *core career*.

Sometimes You Fall Short, and It Ain't So Bad

Like the guy in the story I've just told you, maybe you'll never make all your long-term goals; maybe you'll fall a little short—like he did.

He wanted to write novels; instead he unintentionally became a nonfiction writer. He never became an actor either, but pursuing the acting dream put juice in his life and helped him achieve success with the platform skills he needed as a trainer. Besides, he speaks to audiences large and small around the world and has enhanced thousands of radio and television appearances with these skills. He didn't reach his goals, but he didn't exactly come up with that fistful of mud either.

All those small steps he took at night and on weekends over the years immeasurably enhanced his joy in life and his economic freedom. By striving over the long haul for the big goals in life, even if you fall a little short, you are still way ahead of the game. When it comes to career management, think of stepping-stones and calendars. *You have everything to gain and nothing to lose by making the effort.*

Calendars, Not Clocks

Today you are at the very start of your career and flat broke, but soon enough you will begin to catch up and make some money, and this is when you need to be most aware, because your dreams can get stolen right out from under you.

You live in a world that encourages you to demand instant gratification: "Have it all and have it now; life is tough and you are special; our product will make you somebody better instantly; you deserve it; you owe it to yourself; be better; be thinner; be sexier; be more popular when you buy a *Schmucko* right now!" as the aptly named "boob tube" tells you every eight minutes for five hours every day of your life.

You live with a constant din of consumerism that takes your focus away from the long-term and encourages you to live up to your income and not your dreams. The result, all too often, is that you lose control of your career, and, trapped like a mouse on a paddle wheel, end up too busy running in place to even think about making your dreams for life come true.

Form meaningful goals for your career and your life, and break them down into the many big steps you'll have to take along the way, then *break them down again into smaller and smaller steps*, until there is always some small action that, taken today, will take you a step closer to those distant goals. It's said that the joy of life is in the journey, and these are the ways you can make your life an incredible adventure. You have a right to dream and bring your dreams to life, because this is America and we are a nation that allows you to do that. You start doing this by integrating your dreams into a practical plan of attack that includes the simultaneous pursuit of your *core career*, accompanied, depending on your inclinations, by the pursuit of parallel *entrepreneurial* and *dream careers*.

When you choose a different life path, you may well be criticized and ridiculed. When you make changes in your life in an attempt to grasp what you want from life's all-too-short experience, you will lose people along the way. You will lose people who have been important to you, people who have stood in your way, and people who criticize, don't understand, and don't support your pursuit of meaning and fulfillment. You will walk alone and will need to take strength from your commitment, but pursue your goals with a practical plan of attack and you will gradually replace these people with people who share your goals and values.

Dreams don't materialize out of thin air—you have to work hard and long to make special things happen in your life. You start with a dream, then you determine a plan of action that inches you toward that dream day by day—each new day a tiny step, one after another, after another; 365 tiny steps every year, because your life is not a sprint, it's a marathon. Moving toward your dreams means measuring progress in terms of calendars, not clocks, because the goals that really bring meaning to your life are not achieved overnight. You have the time if you have the commitment, and if you start today.

You have this one life to live. The tools to make it shine are in your hands right now and you understand how to use them. All the tools you need to find this first job and make a success of it are here, and you have learned that they can all be used in other pursuits to make your life more meaningful and to help you achieve real success, however you define it.

When you wake up tomorrow morning, what will you do? Will you watch the lives of others slide by on a screen, or will you work to get what you want out of your life? It's your choice; make it well.

APPENDIX

The *Knock 'em Dead: Secrets & Strategies for First-Time Job Seekers* Brain Trust

Name: **Martin Yate, CPC**
Title: *NY Times* Bestselling Author, *Knock 'em Dead: The Ultimate Job Search Guide*, plus 14 other career books
CEO
Company: Knock 'em Dead
Specialization: Resumes and Coaching
Website: *www.knockemdead.com*
Contact: *martinyate@knockemdead.com*

Name: **Tegan Acree**
Title: Founder
Company: HiringforHope.org
Specialization: Human Resources; Training; Career Management
Website: *www.hiringforhope.org*
Contact: *tacree@hiringforhope.org*

Name: **Leslie Ayres**
Title: Job Search Guru
Company: TheJobSearchGuru.com
Specialization: Executive Recruiter, Straight-Talking Career Coach and Guide to Both Your Inner and Outer Job Search
Website: *www.thejobsearchguru.com*
Contact: *leslie@therealjobguru.com*

Name: **Mark Babbitt**
Title: CEO and Founder
Company: YouTern.com
Specialization: Career Development, Millennial Talent, Internships, Higher Education, Entrepreneurship
Website: *www.youtern.com*
Contact: *mark@youtern.com*

Name: **Jacqui Barrett-Poindexter, MRW, CEIP**
Title: Partner and Chief Career Writer
Company: CareerTrend.net
Specialization: Resume Writing Strategy, Social Media Profile Development
Website: *www.careertrend.net*
Contact: *jacqui@careertrend.net*

Name: **Marjean Bean, CPC**
Title: President
Company: MedIT Staff, LLC
Specialization: Information Technology Recruitment
Website: *www.meditstaff.com*

Name: **Paul R. Bruno, PgMP, PMP**
Title: Program Manager and Host Career Czar radio (retired)
Website: *www.careertrend.com*
Contact: *paulrbruno@cs.co*

Name: **Sultan Camp**
Title: Military Career Transition and Social Network Job Search Specialist
Company: Zeiders Enterprises Inc.
Specialization: Military Transitions and Social Network Business Development
Website: *www.zeiders.com*
Contact: *careersultan@gmail.com*

Name: **Allison Cheston**
Title: Career Connector
Company: Allison Cheston & Associates, LLC
Specialization: Career Advisement for Executives and Young Adults
Website: *www.allisoncheston.com*
Contact: *allison@allisoncheston.com*

Name: **Dr. Larry Chiagouris**
Title: Professor of Marketing and Mentor
Company: Pace University
Specialization: Careers; Personal Branding
Website: *www.thesecrettogettingajobaftercollege.com*
Contact: *lchiagouris@pace.edu*

Name: **Marsha Connolly**
Title: Managing Partner
Company: The New River Group
Specialization: Executive Coaching; Career Management; Professional Identity
                Management
Website: *www.thenewrivergroup.com*
Contact: *marsha.connolly@thenewrivergroup.com*

Name: **Caroline Dowd-Higgins**
Title: Director, Career and Professional Development, Indiana University
                Maurer School of Law; CBS Radio Host
Company: Caroline Dowd-Higgins, LLC
Specialization: Career Reinvention
Website: *www.carolinedowdhiggins.com*
Contact: *cdowd@indiana.edu*

Name: **Dr. Kate Duttro**
Title: Career Coach for Recovering Academics
Company: SeattleCareerChanger.com
Specialization: Career Change for Academics
Website: *www.careerchangeforacademics.com*
Contact: *k.duttro@gmail.com*

Name: **Rich Grant**
Title: Director of Career Services
Company: Thomas College
Specialization: Technology in Job Search (LinkedIn, Twitter)
Website: *www.thomas.edu*
Contact: *career@thomas.edu*

Name: **Meg Guiseppi**
Title: C-level Executive Job-Search Coach
Company: ExecutiveCareerBrand.com
Specialization: Executive Resumes and Coaching
Website: *www.executivecareerbrand.com*
Contact: *meg@executivecareerbrand.com*

Name: **Jessica Hernandez**
Title: President and CEO
Company: GreatResumesFast.com
Specialization: Resume Writing; LinkedIn Profile Development
Website: *www.greatresumesfast.com*
Contact: *info@greatresumesfast.com*

Name: **Sandra Ingemansen, CPRW**
Title: Principal and Chief Resume Designer
Company: ResumeStrategies.com
Specialization: Resume/CV Branding and Writing; Personal Branding;
                   Executive Resume Writing
Website: *www.resume-strategies.com*
Contact: *sandra@resume-strategies.com*

Name: **Marshall J. Karp, MA, NCC, LPC**
Title: Career Counselor
Company: New Career
Specialization: Career Counseling; Job-Search Skills Training
Website: *www.marshalljkarp.com*
Contact: *marshallkarp@hotmail.com*

Name: **Rick Kean, CPC**
Title: Consultant Emeritus
Company: A. M. Hamilton, Inc.
Specialization: Staffing and Staff Training
Website: *www.amhinc.com*
Contact: *rickkean@amhinc.com*

Name: **Scott Keenan**
Title: HR Generalist
Company: Social Media Ninja
Specialization: HR; Social Media; Marketing
Website: *www.educatedandinexperienced.blogspot.com*
Contact: *scottkeenan27@gmail.com*

Name: **Joyce Lain Kennedy**
Title: Syndicated Columnist and Author
Company: Tribune Media Services; For Dummies (Wiley Publishing)
Specialization: Careers
Website: *www.sunfeatures.com*
Contact: *jlk@sunfeatures.com*

Name: **Kevin Kermes**
Title: Founder
Company: Career Attraction
Specialization: Career Management and Transition
Website: *www.careerattraction.com*
Contact: *Kevin@kevinkermes.com*

Name: **Sean Koppelman**
Title: President
Company: The Talent Magnet
Specialization: Recruitment; Executive Search
Website: *www.thetalentmagnet.com*
Contact: *sean@thetalentmagnet.com*

Name: **Roger Lear**
Title: President
Company: OrlandoJobs.com
Specialization: Careers
Website: *www.orlandojobs.com*
Contact: *roger@orlandojobs.com*

Name: **Alexandra Levit**
Title: President and CEO
Company: Inspiration at Work
                   Author, *Blind Spots: The 10 Business Myths You Can't Afford to Believe on Your New Path to Success, They Don't Teach Corporate in College, How'd You Score That Gig?, and New Job, New You*
Specialization: Business; Careers; Workplace
Website: *www.alexandralevit.com*
Contact: *arl@alexandralevit.com*

Name: **Valentino B. Martinez**
Title: President
Company: V.B. Martinez Group
Specialization: Getting and Keeping Careers on Track in the Twenty-First Century
Website: *www.managementconsultants.us*
Contact: *valentino.martinez@gmail.com*

Name: **Karen McGrath, PHR**
Title: Talent Acquisition Manager
Company: Enterprise Rent-A-Car
Specialization: Recruitment
Website: *www.go.enterprise.com*
Contact: *karen.mcgrath@erac.com*

Name: **Kathryn Minshew**
Title: Founder and CEO
Company: The Daily Muse
Website: *www.thedailymuse.com*
Email: *kathryn@thedailymuse.com*

Name: **Hannah Morgan**
Title: Job Search Strategist
Company: CareerSherpa.net
Specialization: Job-Search Strategy
Website: *www.careersherpa.net*
Contact: *hmorgan@careersherpa.net*

Name: **Phyllis Mufson**
Title: Career Coach
Company: Catalyst for Personal and Professional Growth
Specialization: Career Choice; Job Search; Small Business Development
Website: *www.phyllismufson.com*
Contact: *pmufson@comcast.net*

Name: **Carl Nielson**
Title: Principal
Company: Success Discoveries
Specialization: Career Coaching, Executive Coaching
Website: *www.careercoachingforstudents.net*
Contact: *carl@successdiscoveries.com*

Name: **Chris Perry**
Title: Brand and Marketing Generator
Company: Career Rocketeer
Specialization: Personal Branding; Social Media Job Searching; Networking;
                Generation Y Careers
Website: *www.careerrocketeer.com*
Contact: *careerrocketeer@gmail.com*

Name: **Amanda Pouchot**
Title: Founder
Company: The Levo League
Specialization: Elevating Women to Top Executive Positions
Website: *www.levoleague.com*
Contact: *amanda@levoleague.com*

Name: **Jim Rohan**
Title: Senior Partner
Company: J.P. Canon Associates
Specialization: Supply Chain Management; Recruitment
Website: *www.jpcanon.com*
Contact: *jim@jpcanon.com*

Name:	**Lori Ruff**
Title:	CEO, The LinkedIn Diva
Company:	Integrated Alliances
Specialization:	B2B Business Development
Website:	*www.integratedalliances.com*
Contact:	*lruff@integratedalliances.com*

Name:	**Mike Squires**
Title:	Senior Technical Recruiter
Company:	PayPal
Specialization:	Senior Technical Recruitment
Website:	*www.paypal.com*
Contact:	*mikesquires2@gmail.com*

Name:	**Josh Tolan**
Title:	CEO
Company:	SparkHire.com
Specialization:	Video Resumes and Video Interviews
Website:	*www.sparkhire.com*
Contact:	*jtolan@sparkhire.com*

Name:	**Tim Tyrell-Smith**
Title:	Founder
Company:	Tim's Strategy
Specialization:	Careers
Website:	*www.timsstrategy.com*
Contact:	*tim@timsstrategy.com*

Name:	**Joshua Waldman**
Title	Author of *Job Searching with Social Media for Dummies*
Company:	Career Enlightenment
Specialization:	Using Social Media to Find a Great Job
Website:	*www.careerenlightenment.com*
Contact:	*Joshua@careerenlightenment.com*

Name:	**Ron Weisinger**
Title:	Principal
Company:	DevelopmentLINKS Consulting
Specialization:	Human Resources
Website:	*www.linkedin.com/in.ronweisinger*
Contact:	*ronweisinger@comcast.net*

Name:	**Denise Wilkerson, RN, CPC**
Title:	Director of Executive Search
Company:	Global Edge Recruiting
Specialization:	Medical Devices; Biotechnology; Pharmaceuticals-Sales Marketing; Management
Website:	*www.globaledgerecruiting.com*
Contact:	*denise@globaledgerecruiting.com*

Name:	**Leslie Zaikis**
Title:	Director of Business Development
Company:	The Levo League
Specialization:	Generation Y Women and Job Search
Website:	*www.levoleague.com*
Contact:	*leslie.zaikis@gmail.com*

INDEX